LEV SHEININ

DIARY
OF A CRIMINOLOGIST

LEV SHEININ

University Press of the Pacific
Honolulu, Hawaii

Diary of a Criminologist

by
Lev Sheinin

ISBN: 1-4102-1039-1

Copyright © 2004 by University Press of the Pacific

University Press of the Pacific
Honolulu, Hawaii
http://www.universitypressofthepacific.com

CONTENTS

A FEW WORDS ABOUT MYSELF

Many are the paths which lead a writer to literature. Mine began in the Criminal Investigation Department.

Today, March 25, 1956, the day of my, alas, fiftieth birthday, I look back on how it all began. I recall Moscow that frosty February day in 1923 when I, then a student of the Bryusov Institute of Literature and Art and a member of the Komsomol, was urgently summoned to the Krasnopresnensky District Komsomol Committee.

Moscow of 1923, Moscow of my youth, I shall never forget you! Closing my eyes, I can see your snow-covered boulevards, narrow Tverskaya Street with the Iverskaya Chapel of Our Lady at Okhotny Ryad, the groaning trams that were few and far between, the sleepy cabbies at the crossroads, the horses munching oats from their feed-bags, the Mosselprom salesgirls (it was the first Soviet company) in their cute gold-stitched uniform caps, selling chocolates and "Ira" cigarettes from trays (all that was left, they used to say, of the old world); I can see the smoky tea-room at Zatsepa Market where shopkeepers and students, cabbies and Zatsepa butchers, market pickpockets and full-bosomed, red-cheeked milkmaids waiting for suburban trains from Paveletsky Station came in to warm up. I can see your railway stations, crowded students' dormitories, the merry, all-night queues at the Moscow Art Theatre box-office and "The Great Silent" cinema on Tverskoi Boulevard; and, true enough, the cinema *was* silent in those days.

It was a strange time, and Moscow itself was strange. Turbulent Sukharevka with its rows of stands, stalls and shops coexisted with the Komsomol clubrooms in the former merchants' mansions; the freshly painted signs outside the shops and offices of the first Nepmen* and the Pokrovsky Workers' High School auditoriums in Mokhovaya Street where yesterday's lathe-operators, fitters and engine-drivers were cramming for college entrance exams; the

* From NEP—New Economic Policy.

huge black sign outside the Moscow Anarchists' Club in Tverskaya ("Anarchy Is the Mother of Order") and the weird murals in the "Pegasus' Stable" café on the corner of Strastnaya Square where Imagists read their works to a motley and none-too-sober audience.

The young people at the Komsomol clubs sang the popular "We're the Young Guard of Workers and Peasants," studied Esperanto to hasten the world revolution through a unified language for the proletarians of all countries; they hacked away with fervour at the granite of knowledge and hated the Nepmen whom they were temporarily forced to tolerate.

Meanwhile, all sorts of derelicts had crawled out of every nook and cranny; these were professional card-sharpers and arrogant cocottes, speculators with greed-flushed faces and silent elegant white-slavers, bandits with aristocratic affectations and former aristocrats-turned-bandits, erotomaniacs and just plain thieves of every shape, size and colour.

Each passing day brought its crop of short-lived, shady "concerns" and "anonymous stock companies," which lasted just long enough to swindle the recent government establishments with which they had signed contracts for construction and deliveries of all sorts of goods.

The first foreign concessions had sprung up: lumber mills, pencil and hosiery factories.

The concessionaires, the Hammers, Petersons, Van Bergs and what not, who had established permanent headquarters in Moscow and Leningrad, had pretty mistresses, secretly bought up furs and currency, ancient Rublyov icons and Vologda laces, priceless paintings and crystal-ware, sending it all back home on the quiet, and, at the same time, went mad over ballet and ballerinas. They sighed over the fate of the "poor Russian people caught unawares by the Communists who refuted the normal, human order of things, but who were apparently coming to their senses at last."

I entered the District Komsomol Office at the appointed hour, unable to guess why I had been summoned so urgently. When I asked Osipov, the head of the organizational section, he smiled mysteriously and said that Sasha Gramp, the District Secretary, would answer that question.

I was a member of the District Committee and knew Sasha well. Osipov and I entered his office together.

"Hello, Lev," he said. "Take a seat. We've a serious matter to discuss."

I sat down opposite him. He told me that the Moscow Komsomol Committee had passed a resolution to mobilize a group of long-standing members of the Komsomol for public service. Since I had been a member from 1919 I was included in the list.

"We're devilishly in need of revenue inspectors and criminal investigators," Gramp continued, puffing away at an enormous pipe he actually hated, but smoked to look more impressive. "The revenue inspectors are in charge of collecting taxes from the Nepmen, but the Nepmen sidle up to them in all sorts of ways and the budget suffers in the end. Understand?"

"Yes. But where do I come in?" I asked uncertainly.

"We can't have the budget suffer!" Gramp retorted, puffing away menacingly. "But there's an even greater need for investigators than for revenue inspectors. Do you know that two-thirds of the investigators at the Moscow Regional Court are non-Party members, and that some of them even held the same jobs in tsarist times? The Revolution should have its own Sherlock Holmeses. Understand?"

"But, Sasha, I never wanted to be a revenue inspector nor a criminal investigator!" I objected carefully. "I've no head for figures; and as for Sherlock Holmes, all I remember about him is that he smoked a pipe, lived in Baker Street and played the violin. I think he invented some sort of deductive method, had a friend, a Doctor Watson, who always managed to ask stupid questions at the right time just to give Holmes a chance to come up with a clever answer. But that's not the main thing. I'm studying at the Literature Institute and intend to devote my life to literature, and...."

"And you're a fool!" Gramp interrupted. "What does the Revolution care about your petty desires? Besides, if you've decided to become a writer, what can be better than starting out immediately as a revenue inspector, or, better still, as a criminal investigator? You'll have all the plots, characters and human drama you want—that's where you'll find literature, my friend! But that's not the main thing either. The Soviet Government needs revenue inspectors and investigators; and we must supply them. You're one of those we're supplying, and that's all there's to it! Put a period right there, and an exclamation mark too, if you like, but no question marks! Where would you rather work: at the Regional Finance Department or the Regional Court?"

"You've just said there'd be no question marks, so why contradict yourself?"

"Comrade Sheinin," Gramp said icily, "this is a Party mobilization! You have till evening to decide where you'd rather work. Then come back and tell me. I'll see you this evening, Byron!"

Gramp called me Byron because I had a mass of hair then, which has since, alas, disappeared, and wore a soft collar.

That is how I became a Moscow Regional Court investigator. It is difficult to understand, of course, how a teenager with no legal education could have been appointed a criminal investigator, but that is exactly what happened. All this took place in the early years of the Soviet Government, when life itself pressed for the promotion of new cadres in every field. The situation was especially critical in the legal field. The Soviet procurator's office was established only a year before, on the suggestion of V. I. Lenin. The Soviet Government then introduced the people's and regional courts to take the place of the revolutionary tribunals of the first years. Criminal and Legal codes had been adopted, and justice could now rely on the law, and not only on "revolutionary consciousness."

I was unhappy about being mobilized, fearing that my new job would interfere with my studies and above all with my career as a writer. Little did I realize then that a writer's best school is life itself and that no college education, or even a degree in literature, could take its place.

Nor did I understand at the time that there is much in common between a writer and a criminal investigator, the latter coming constantly in contact with diverse characters, conflicts and dramas. No investigator can foretell the case life will dump on to his desk in the morning. But whatever it may be—robbery, jealousy murder, embezzlement or bribery—it is the people behind the crime that matter most; each has his own character, emotions and fate. The investigator will never see what lies behind the crime unless he understands the psychology of the people involved. He will never really grasp the case he is duty-bound to grasp without delving into the inner sanctum of each defendant, into the complicated and often curious tangle of events, coincidences, vices, bad habits and connections, weaknesses and passions.

That is why an investigator's job always depends on his understanding of psychology and human nature, something it shares with the work of a writer, who must also look into the souls of his characters, marking their joys and sorrows, their successes and misfortunes, their weaknesses and mistakes.

Chance, which had made me an investigator, thus also determined my fate as a writer.

Gramp was quite right. There were many non-Party members and even several "tsarist" specialists among the Moscow investigators. Of the latter, it was Ivan Snitovsky, a sturdy, sixty-year-old Ukrainian with a mischievous face and dark laughing eyes who made the greatest impression upon me. He had had thirty years of experience as a court investigator and was handling major cases of the Moscow Judicial Council prior to the Revolution. Unlike many of his colleagues, Snitovsky did not emigrate after the Revolution. Despite his noble birth, he accepted the ideals of the Revolution, pinning his faith on them. A great expert in his field, he was enthusiastic about his life's work and always ready to help his younger colleagues, many of whom had been factory or Party workers.

After receiving my appointment to the Regional Court, I was assigned as a probationer to Snitovsky and another senior investigator, Minai Laskin.

Laskin had begun his career as a criminal investigator while still a student in 1918, shortly after the Revolution. He was then assigned to a Revolutionary Tribunal. Short, vivacious and shrewd, he, too, was devoted to his profession and was considered one of the best investigators of the Moscow Regional Court.

The Presidium of the Regional Court, naturally, were worried about my age and demanded that these two men take me in tow for six months to see what would come of "this risky experiment," as the chairman of the court called it.

When I first entered Snitovsky's office (he had been told of my assignment and of his new responsibilities) he rose quickly and approached me with a smile.

"Well, well. How do you do, young man," he said, shaking my hand. "I'm ready to bet you're not yet eighteen, are you?"

"I will be soon," I answered, drawn somehow to this friendly, good-natured man. I liked his dark, clean-cut features and large brown eyes.

"There, there! You've nothing to blush about! Youth is a handicap remedied with each passing hour. Come, sit down in this armchair, relax, and let's get to know each other."

An hour later, without my noticing it, this kind smiling man had found out nearly everything there was to know about me. It was only afterwards that I was really able to appreciate his faculty to sift things out, avoiding direct questions and piercing looks, getting at what he wanted in a detached and friendly manner, chatting, laughing, joking and putting his companion quite at ease.

Needless to say, I worshipped the man by the end of our first talk and meant to do everything to win his approval and faith in my budding abilities.

I met Laskin, my second patron, on the same day. We discovered that we were both from the town of Toropets, Pskov Region, where I had lived most of my life and joined the Komsomol and that he knew my elder sisters well: they had been at secondary school when he was in his last semester in another secondary school of the town.

My sponsors took their assignment—to see "what would come of the experiment"—very seriously, and I am much indebted to both of them. After six months I was to be examined by the Regional Court Certifying Commission whose verdict would determine my future.

The guidance of my two intelligent and conscientious teachers who had kindled my interest and respect for the profession and the fact that the articles of the Criminal and Legal codes I was studying came to life every day before my eyes in the persons of the defendants made me absorb the essentials of crime detection avidly.

One day, about three months later, Snitovsky laid an arm around my shoulders and, looking me straight in the eye, said in a quiet and very earnest tone:

"May I drop dead, my boy, if you don't make good some day. True, you did not graduate from a lyceum and never, alas, contended for a legal position in court, being as green as a cucumber besides, but I'll still make an investigator of you, in spite of God and Man! See if I don't!"

Then he turned to Laskin, who had just entered the room:

"Minai, pillar of wisdom that you are, tell

me the truth and only the truth! Will he ever investigate a major case or not?"

"You're killing me," Laskin said smiling. "Can't you tell he'll make good by looking at *me*? After all, he's from Toropets too! There's nothing the people of Toropets have not been able to do from the day Alexander Nevsky got married in their town."

Six months later I took my examination. Degtyaryov, the glum bearded and very stern old Chairman of the Regional Court Certifying Commission, quizzed me mercilessly on all the chapters and articles of the Criminal, Legal, Civil and Labour codes, grumbling as he heard my answers, and remarking:

"That's no child's play for you, my dear fellow. Now, tell me what the presumption of innocence principle is all about and with what sauce you serve it."

"In criminal law the presumption of innocence means that the court and the investigating bodies must proceed on the assumption that the defendant is innocent. Which means that he is not compelled to prove his innocence, but that the investigation, if they have sufficient evidence, must prove his guilt. A person is considered innocent of a crime until his guilt has been legally established beyond doubt."

"Hm.... Well, that's not as simple as you think! Now, be good enough to tell me how minors are questioned."

"Minors are questioned by an investigator alone or in the presence of their parents or guardians. The investigator must refrain from leading questions to avoid suggesting the answers he wants from the child. On the other hand, the child's description of a criminal, of his behaviour, clothing, etc., must be heard attentively, as children are extremely observant and their perception is keen. In questioning a child, one must speak to him seriously, as if he were an adult, and never use baby-talk, as this will put him on his guard. If a child is being questioned as the victim in a case of corruption or seduction, the investigator must put his questions with extreme care to avoid corruption of the child or causing additional trauma."

"Hm. That's right. Well, my boy, we'll give you an investigator's certificate, though you're only a sparrow yourself. Remember once and for all: always keep calm! Principles of criminal procedure is not a thing to be learnt from a book—you must understand it with your heart.

When questioning a person, bear in mind that it's a routine matter for you, but that he may remember it for the rest of his life. Then remember, too, that the first version of a case is not necessarily the correct one. And, most important, when questioning thieves and murderers, violators and swindlers, never forget that they were born into this world as naked as you and I, and may yet become as good citizens as we. And if you should ever get sick of your by no means easy job, or begin to lose faith in people—then run off, my boy, run! Don't stay at it another day, but hand in your resignation, saying you are no longer fit to be an investigator."

Then old man Degtyaryov, that forbidding old Bolshevik and former political prisoner so highly respected in the court, but feared for his sharp tongue, lashing judgement and intolerance of misdemeanours committed by members of the legal profession (he was also chairman of the Regional Court Disciplinary Collegium), arose, shook my hand, looked at me searchingly and smiled, which was something I had never seen him do before.

When I came out I found Snitovsky and Laskin pacing the corridor. The suspense had been too great for my dear teachers and both had hurried over to the Regional Court where they waited for me, cursing the "beard," as Degtyaryov was called, for giving their fledgling a hard time and trying to fail him.

When they saw my flushed, happy face they heaved a sigh of relief and showered me with questions as to how and how long that "bearded tiger and scorpion" had tormented me.

This very same "tiger" followed my every step closely in the years to come, until the day I was transferred to Leningrad. Though I never knew it, he studied all the cases I submitted to the Regional Court. Often, too, he invited me to his home for tea where, with the same lowering look, and coughing into his greying beard, he hammered home the "Ten Commandments" of a Soviet legal worker.

But I no longer feared his gloominess, his angry coughing, nor his beard, for I had come to understand this wise kind man who had led an honest but very difficult life and whom I shall remember to my dying day.

There were many others who felt the same as I. When Ivan Degtyaryov died of a heart attack several years later, the whole of the Regional Court followed his coffin to the cemetery; standing there beside Snitovsky and Laskin, I saw through my tears that they, too, were weeping, as were so many others, among them not a few whom the late chairman of the Disciplinary Collegium had "rubbed the wrong way" for various misdemeanours.

It was then, too, that I thought of my own mistake, one for which I had come up before the Disciplinary Collegium and which I feared would bring the curtain down on my job as an investigator–a job I had really come to love.

This happened to me in one of my first cases. It had to do with some ancient dinars and, strangely enough, with "Admiral Nelson." I have described this amusing and instructive incident in the story *Dinars with Holes.*

* * *

Having passed the certifying commission's examination, I was sent to Orekhovo-Zuyevo as a people's investigator. I spent six months in this Moscow Region town, investigating my first cases: horse-stealing, embezzlement in a co-operative, a suicide caused by unrequited love and manslaughter at a village wedding. I conscientiously kept to the investigator's "Ten Commandments" taught by Degtyaryov, Snitovsky and Laskin, remembering that a cool head was the main thing, that the art of cross-examination lay in the ability to *listen* as well as to *question*, that the first version was not always the correct one, that a person being interrogated would be nervous, whether guilty or not, and that, as even Dostoyevsky once so truly said, it is as impossible to build a horse with a hundred rabbits, as to produce irrefutable proof of the defendant's guilt with a hundred small and unconnected bits of evidence.

Six months later I was unexpectedly transferred to Moscow and again assigned to the investigating department of the Regional Court. Several days later I made my first mistake, one that caused me much worry and anxiety. It concerned the case of the jeweller Visotsky.

There was rain and mud in the spring of 1924. I lived in Zatsepa across the Moskva River then and had to travel a long way to my place of work in Stoleshnikov Street. I decided that I needed new galoshes and bought a magnificent pair with a red imitation plush lining which, for some reason, were called "general's galoshes."

Next morning I arrived at the office very proud of my buy. I set my magnificent, shining galoshes with the Mephistophelian lining in the corner and took my place at the desk in my little office, raising my head from time to time to look happily at what I considered a luxurious acquisition.

Snitovsky was working on the Visotsky case at that time. There was evidence that the jeweller had been buying diamonds for a foreign concessionaire and helping to smuggle them across the border. Snitovsky had put a lot of effort into gathering his evidence on the criminal activities and connections of this very shrewd man. There was enough proof, finally, to obtain a warrant for the jeweller's arrest, but as Snitovsky was busy with several other cases, he told me to summon Visotsky, cross-examine him, read him the warrant for his arrest and send him to jail.

Visotsky was summoned and arrived punctually. He was a man of about forty, elegantly, though a bit foppishly dressed, with a mouthful of gold teeth and a sugary smile which, it seemed to me, he had assumed for ever and perhaps even went to bed with.

I began the cross-examination. The jeweller was fond of what he considered to be the high society manner and bored me for two hours with such phrases as: "Permit me to call your attention to the fact," "if you permit me," "not desiring to tire you, nevertheless," "if you'll be so kind as to take into consideration."

Having finished the cross-examination, I presented him with the warrant for his arrest, based on Article 145 of the Criminal Code, which in exceptional cases allowed the arrest of a suspect without presenting him with charges for a period not exceeding two weeks. Then I patiently listened to his protestations. He said he was "absolutely aghast," "quite flabbergasted," and viewed the matter as "an impossible, if you permit me to be frank, misunderstanding," which he hoped "with every fibre of his soul" would soon be cleared up.

All the while this shrewd and experienced rogue remained completely at ease, apparently counting on wriggling out of it, especially since, on Snitovsky's suggestion, I had not presented him with all the evidence; the real reason for charges against him had been intentionally withheld.

Visotsky signed a paper stating that he had read the warrant for his arrest; I then locked the case up in my safe and went to tell the executive secretary to summon a convoy and the prison van. When I entered the secretary's office I found him standing on the window-sill, a rat scurrying round the room. I hate rats myself, but his screaming made me laugh and I began to soothe him. He would not come down until the rat had ducked into a hole. I then spent some time telling him what was to be done.

Imagine my shock when I returned to my office to find that both Visotsky and my new galoshes were gone.

He had left the following note on my desk: "I hope that you, dear sir, will not think that a person of my breeding is capable of stealing your galoshes. No, I have merely borrowed them as it is quite wet outside and I, with no small thanks to you, now have a rather long journey ahead of me. Best wishes! Visotsky."

Horrified, I ran to Snitovsky.

He glanced at the note, picked up the receiver and called MUR.* Snitovsky had discovered the name of Visotsky's mistress, though the jeweller had no inkling of this. Snitovsky asked MUR to keep an eye on her apartment, guessing correctly that before leaving Moscow Visotsky would certainly come to say goodbye to his sweetheart, whose existence he, a married man, took great pains to keep secret.

Snitovsky hung up the receiver and turned to me:

* MUR—Moscow Criminal Investigation Bureau.

"Well, Lev, I m positive that scoundrel will be arrested, but I hope that this sad experience with your galoshes will be a lesson to you and teach you that an investigator must always be on his toes."

I was upset all day until the MUR agents brought Visotsky in the evening. Snitovsky had correctly guessed that he would go to see his sweetheart. As self-possessed as ever, the jeweller removed my galoshes and said with a flourish: "Pardon, but it was extremely damp, and, if you permit me to say so, I cannot stand such weather. Once again—*mille* pardons!"

I stayed on in Moscow until 1927, when I was made senior criminal investigator of the Leningrad Regional Court.

Three years later I was transferred back to Moscow again and appointed an investigator of major cases. Then, in 1935, I was appointed Chief of the Investigating Department of the Procurator's Office of the U.S.S.R., where I worked until January 1, 1950, when I decided to dedicate myself completely to writing.

Thus, I spent twenty-seven years of my life working on criminal cases. Naturally, this was a determining factor in my choice of subject matter, beginning with my first story *Kirill Lavrinenko's Career*, published in the magazine *Court's in Session!* in 1928.

This was the first of the stories which came to be known as *Diary of a Criminologist*, and which appeared in the newspapers *Pravda* and *Izvestia* and in several magazines. The collection was published in book form in 1938. The first part of the book was written in the bustle of investigation work, with new crimes constantly demanding immediate action. Some of the stories and sketches were obviously rough, having been written during my very few hours of leisure. Had I written them now, I would have certainly worked over them more, but I had no time for it then.

In preparing this book for publication, my first impulse was to rewrite several of the old stories; then I felt a certain urge to leave them exactly as they were. It is difficult to explain this feeling. Perhaps it was a subconscious desire to preserve those first efforts of my physical and literary youth, with all its joys and sorrows, discoveries and mistakes. Perhaps, also, it was the subconscious fear of "shoving away" the sincerity of these stories by refurbishing them and adding new psychological details. It may be, too, that without admitting it to myself I preserved the original version of those early stories to compare them with others written more maturely, and thus get a clearer view of my progress as a writer. Or perhaps it was all these reasons put together.

In short, I have kept all of the stories in the shape in which they were first written, dating each and changing the names of the charac- ters who in real life have long since served their sentences and become honest citizens. I wish them well with all my heart and do not want to darken their lives with recollections of events that belong to the past and should be left there.

In combating crime in those far-off days, a new approach, the one of "remaking" profes- sional criminals into honest, hard-working citizens, was developed.

In my years as a criminologist I came to understand that by appealing to a man's better nature, even if he were a criminal one, was al- most certain to establish a bond of under- standing. I realized that unless the investigator established such a bond, he would never be able to diagnose a given crime effectively, just as the physician unable to establish contact with his patient would never be able to diag- nose his illness correctly. Through many years of observation I reached the psychological contact theory, which I call the "mutual trust system." Obviously, this was not accomplished overnight, nor did I rely only on my own experience, but took into account the work of my colleagues as well. The reader will find many of their names in this book, and I feel it my duty to express fraternal gratitude for much that they have taught me and helped me to find at the start of my work in criminal detection.

I am convinced that the mutual trust system can be very broadly applied, and that it is a very effective means of education.

Referring to *Crime and Punishment* in his work on Dostoyevsky, Academician A. F. Koni, an outstanding Russian criminologist, wrote: "The characters he created in his novel will live for ever in their artistic impact. They will never die as examples of the lofty ability to discover the 'living soul' beneath the coarsest, gloomiest and ugliest shell, and, in uncovering it, compassionately to reveal the now softly glowing, now brightly burning flame of conciliation. . . ."

These remarkable words of Academician Koni have acquired special meaning in our time, in our socialist society.

In the hardest years of the struggle against the counter-revolution, F. E. Dzerzhinsky found the time and the will to organize the first children's communes and work colonies, to create children's homes for waifs and to establish a system of re-education-through-work in penal institutions.

These great social and psychological problems prompted such outstanding Soviet works as those written by A. Makarenko, books which, without exaggeration, have stirred the world and won respectful interest and acclaim even from the bourgeois literary critics, pedagogues and criminologists. Gorky often wrote with pride and admiration of the remarkable results obtained by this method in the re-education of former criminals, and especially the juvenile delinquents.

Reviewing the road I have travelled, I recall everything I saw, heard and came to understand while working as an investigator, things which helped me immeasurably as a writer. I look back on my years as a criminologist with a warm feeling of gratitude, for I am indebted to them for many of my themes, situations, characters and plots.

Among these many themes, the closest to my heart is that of correcting the criminal.

I am convinced that as long as a criminal is alive and breathing, capable of observing, and thinking, it is never too late for him to return to our large and happy Soviet family under our social system, if only he has been given the necessary qualified help.

If these notes should prove one such avenue of help, and if my readers come to share my convictions, I shall be happy in the knowledge that I did not embark in vain upon the difficult but gratifying path of writing.

DIARY OF A CRIMINOLOGIST

DINARS WITH HOLES

Before telling of this curious case, the events of which took place at the very beginning of my career, I should like to relate the story I was told by a thief, one of the first from whom I was to learn of the unexpected response that confidence will sometimes arouse in a criminal's soul. The criminal in question, a tall, well-built fellow, had a slightly sleepy and unusually kind face for his profession, with round eyes that seemed to regard the world with constant bewilderment. He had had several previous convictions and was known to the underworld and to MUR as "the Lout."

Asking for a cigarette that day, after the interrogation was over, he lit it and said:

"Thanks for the tobacco and our nice talk. But one good turn deserves another, as they say, and so with your permission, I'll tell you about something that happened in my life, something which, I would say, was very queer."

"Please do," I agreed wondering why the Lout suddenly looked embarrassed.

"As you know, I've been in the business a long time," he said, his embarrassment growing. "But I've never stooped to the sticky stuff and never will. I always work at night, waiting around in a dark alley for someone to pass by, preferably a lady. Well, I walk over, say hello, and relieve her of her fur coat, or watch, or bag, for what-have-you. But I always do this in a gentlemanly way, because I'm a cultured person. I like the cinema and can't stand vulgarity, which I consider a belch of the old world. That's why you can take my word when I say that I never laid a finger on anyone. You can see for yourself that my kind of fingers are better kept away from such things."

The Lout smiled and extended a huge brawny paw. Then he sighed and continued:

"It's no use lying, my conscience never bothered me and I lived a happy life, keeping my feet dry, as they say, until I tripped up on a little lady."

"Was it love?" I asked, anticipating a tale of unrequited love, like so many others I had heard from criminals before.

"Ah, no. It was my conscience," he answered. "It happened one night in a side street of Devichye Polye. I was in a dark corner, waiting for a nibble. It was a frosty night, pitch dark, and not a soul in sight. Suddenly, I heard a door slam and a girl rushed out of a house. She was quite young and slender and had on a fur coat. Probably scared by all that black emptiness around, she put her collar up and began to run looking back to see if anyone was chasing her, her high heels clicking on the pavement. Well, I thought, that's real luck, and it's up to me to nationalize that fur coat. I detached myself from the gate and headed straight for her. She saw me coming and ran right up to me. Then, imagine, she grabbed my arm and cried in a pitiful voice: 'Oh, Mister, please excuse me, but I'm so frightened! There's not a soul in sight. Won't you take me to a cab?' I'd rather she had knifed me! I still can't understand what happened, but I crooked my arm and muttered: 'Don't you worry, I'll protect you.' 'Ah,' she said, 'I'm so grateful! I knew right away that you were a real gentleman.' And off we went.

My heart was pounding and I felt hot all over. I didn't know what was happening to me, but I just couldn't get down to business. I tell you, I just couldn't. What a situation! Anyway, I saw her to a sleigh, helped her in, bundled her in the fur wrap and wished her a good journey. See what confidence can do to a man!"

"But you still continued mugging after that, didn't you?" I asked.

"I couldn't work for about three days; then I went out again. But I'll tell you, it was as if something had cracked inside of me. I couldn't rob women and was fed up with everything. I sort of lost my touch and my faith in myself. After I'm convicted now and do my stretch, I'll go straight. I've had enough! It's just like I was shell-shocked that night."

There was such sadness in his eyes that I knew he meant what he said.

I was a people's investigator of the Krasnopresnensky District in Moscow at the time. My district included all of Gorky Street, Krasnaya Presnya, and the adjacent streets and alleys. MUR was then located at Bolshoi Gnezdnikovsky Street and was also in my district. This accounted for my close friendship with many of the staff and especially with Nikolai Osipov, Chief of the First MUR Brigade, and his assistant, Georgi Tylner, both in their thirties.

The First MUR Brigade was in charge of investigating murders and armed robberies, and was the very heart of the Criminal Investigation Bureau. If one recalls how many professional criminals there were at that time, it will be clear that my friends were busy night and day.

They were both keen criminologists, who liked their difficult jobs and knew them well. Osipov was thin and blond, always neatly dressed, and his clever grey eyes were quick and sharp. He was a good judge of human nature, knew the psychology and jargon of the underworld and was also an ardent motor-cyclist.

As I was very young and just starting my career, my friendship with them was both pleasant and useful. I learned much from them and listened excitely to their stories of crime, of accidents and discoveries.

I was often present when Osipov or Tylner interrogated a criminal. I could hardly understand what they were talking about at first. There was so much underworld slang and professional terminology in the questions and answers that I almost thought they were speaking in some foreign tongue.

The Moscow underworld knew both men well. The criminals hated the MUR as a rule, but regarded Osipov and Tylner with respect and, strange as it may seem, even felt a certain fondness for them; everyone knew they were "on the level," and their fairness and courage were common knowledge.

Besides, Osipov, who knew this strange world well, never ridiculed prisoners or humiliated them; he kept to the letter of the law, made no special allowances, but always spoke to them as man to man and with great tact.

Tylner was a polite, well-mannered and handsome man known for his phenomenal memory. As they said in MUR, he had the entire Moscow underworld "in his head," and remembered practically all the names, aliases, identity marks and previous convictions of the Moscow recidivists. The latter were well aware of this and often said it was better "to keep out of Baron Tylner's sight, and not to try to peddle goulash to him," meaning that it was impossible to fake one's identity as far as he was concerned.

There is still an attractive, tiled house in Blagoveshchensky Street in which the families of the government officials used to live. One of its old residents was a People's Commissar named S.

On a night in July, when S. and his family were in the country, thieves broke into his apartment and, among various household things, took a large leather pouch containing a collection of ancient coins which he had amassed over many years.

There was an awful uproar. The men of the Second MUR Brigade, in charge of burglaries, realized it would be difficult to catch the thief and that the case promised nothing but trouble. Stepanov, head of the Second Brigade, tall, imposing, extremely courteous and very diplomatic, was so upset that he smoked a cigarette out of turn. (His whole life was carefully planned; he never rushed, considering hastiness bad for his health, which he valued highly. He was known to the underworld as "Molasses.") He sat looking at his shining manicured nails and then said softly to his assistant Krotov:

"Misha, wouldn't you say this was an expert theft, and not a simple one? Hm?"

Shrewd Krotov looked at his chief in surprise, but grasped the situation in a flash (simple thefts, according to Article 108 of the Criminal Code, were investigated by MUR, while expert thefts were handed to people's investigators), and immediately began to swear by all that was holy that never in his life had he seen a more expert theft.

According to the letter of the law, burglaries and thefts in which special housebreaking tools had been used were considered expert thefts, but this was not the case in this instance, as the thief or thieves had gained access through the window and thus undoubtedly belonged to the category known as "window men." That is why Stepanov reacted to Krotov's protestations with a wry look.

"Misha, I can't seem to remember a special Krotov interpretation of expert theft in Article 162. It's window-job, my boy, isn't it?"

Krotov stopped short, lowered his eyes, but would not give in.

"Ah, but they opened the window with special tools," he said significantly, his lucid eyes fixed on his chief.

"Is that so? I can't seem to recall that either," Stepanov answered. "Unless, of course, you can prove that fingers are special tools, my friend."

"Fingers have nothing to do with it," Krotov said excitedly. "There is every indication that the window was forced with a chisel and that the lock was broken. There are special tools and breaking in for you."

"You don't say? Well, that's too bad. It's certainly a shame to part with such an interesting case, but the law comes first, Misha," sighed Stepanov lighting another unscheduled cigarette, this time with obvious relief. "No, my friend, there's nothing we can do. Send the case to the people's investigator, according to Article 108. And prepare the papers."

Next day I received a case with an accompanying note written in a very flowery style. In it Krotov described with great temperament and emotion "the use of special tools, such as a chisel, which fact could be deduced from the protocol of an examination of the window," and "typical traces of housebreaking, indicated by the broken window-lock, attached herewith as material evidence."

An hour after I received the case, Stepanov phoned and inquired after my health and my work in a most courteous and touching manner. He praised the weather and Tatyana Bakh's singing in *The Queen of Czardas*, advising me strongly to see it; and then, at the end of our very long talk, said casually:

"By the way, I hope you won't mind, but we've sent you a little case. It's not up to us, the law comes first. You can be sure we'll do our best to help you wherever possible. Would you be so kind as to send me a note saying you've accepted the case? I need it for my books. I'll send Krotov over for it."

As I hung up, I did not realize what the shrewd Molasses had dumped on my trusting head and gave Krotov, who, surprisingly, arrived in record time, the note he asked for.

It became all too clear the following morning, when Sheverdin, the Regional Procurator, a wise and kind old man who, like Degtyaryov, had been a political prisoner under the tsarist government, phoned to say I was to come to his office immediately and bring the case of the burglary at Blagoveshchensky Street.

Before starting out, I looked through the case carefully and noticed how flimsy the "expert" clues were, but by then I was tied hand and foot by my resolution accepting the case and by the note which Krotov had carried off like a wolf carries off a lamb.

Sheverdin listened to my report and looked through the case—which at this point was made up, in the main, of documents showing how MUR had passed it on to me. He smiled and said:

"Well, well, this is very interesting. Stepanov, being no fool, palmed it off, and you, my downy-cheeked boy, were in a great rush to accept it. You are now at that happy but dangerous age when you have already learned *what to do*, but have not yet learned *what not to do*. Stepanov has learned them both, and especially the second. What shall we do now? It's practically impossible to track down a window thief. S. is foaming at the mouth and bellowing like a bull, demanding that we report to him. Let's start out, my child. I foresee unpleasantness! I know the victim's character only too well."

When we entered and Sheverdin introduced me as the inspector in charge of the case, S., a small, stout, greying man, was in a highly irritated state.

"Oh, so this is the inspector?" he growled. "Well, now I can see why all sorts of thieves break into the apartments of People's Commissars and get away with it! Comrade Sheverdin, are you running a kindergarten or a Procurator's Office?"

Sheverdin answered politely but with great

dignity that though I was young I was a prom-
ising investigator and worked well, and as
for the Commissar's question, he, Sheverdin,
for one, did not intend to ask the Commissar
just how old his inspectors were.

S. flared up and began shouting that he
would complain to the Government if the criminal were not apprehended in three days,
that he didn't give a damn for the other stolen
things, but that he was a numismatist and
had spent his life collecting ancient coins, that
his extraordinary collection included dinars
with holes dating to the times of Alexander
the Great, that this was no joke and that he
could not understand the Regional Procurator's inertia, that he had no faith in investigators just out of the cradle and, in general, was
not going to wait longer than three days,
counting from that very minute.

Sheverdin had also reached the boiling
point, but finding it impossible to carry on the
conversation in the presence of a young investigator, he asked me to wait for him outside.
Half an hour later he came out in a purple rage
and carried me off to his office.

On the way and at the office later the old
man berated S. for his "high-handed manner"
and "unsocialist arrogance." True enough, sev-

eral years later S. was relieved of his post as a People's Commissar as unfit for the job.

Stammering from nervousness and mentally cursing shrewd Stepanov and my own short-sightedness, I told Sheverdin that, as he had correctly noted, housebreaking cases were the most difficult and that the percentage solved was very low; that I, as an investigator, had no detectives or contacts at my disposal and could not take it upon myself to solve the case by pure deduction.

It was decided that I go to MUR and get Stepanov to mobilize all his forces to help solve the accursed case.

A vain hope! When I spoke to him, he told me frankly that he was very pessimistic about the outcome.

"You must understand, my dear man," he said, "that it was a window job, and that the burglar had no idea of whom he was robbing. A capable professional burglar would never have set foot in that house! The thief was a beginner, and certainly not a recidivist. You'll never find him! Krotov and I investigated the possibilities before floating the case your way."

To this Stepanov added a sweet, most sympathetic smile.

I went to see my friends of the First Brigade quite disheartened. Questioning me closely, Osipov shook his head: "Damn Molasses! He always finds someone to get the chestnuts out of the fire."

The boys of the First Brigade disliked Stepanov and his "diplomatic methods." Osipov saw that I was in trouble and wanted to help, but as an experienced inspector he saw, too, that the case was practically hopeless. He had to agree with Stepanov: a "real, professional thief" would never have broken into a Commissar's apartment, not on his life!

"I don't know how to help you, my boy," he said. "Judging by everything that coin collector won't give you any peace. There's nothing worse than getting involved with a collector. They're usually all maniacs. Dinars with holes in them! If they hadn't any holes, you'd be better off, perhaps, but with holes you're just out of luck!"

At that moment Osipov's secretary came in and handed him a coded message from Odessa. He read the telegram, looked thoughtful, then brightened suddenly and handed it to me with the expression of one who has unexpectedly found a ray of hope in what seemed an impossible situation.

"Read this, old man," he said. "It has some bearing on the case. You were born under a lucky star."

I grabbed the telegram, read it over twice, but could find nothing to show that I was any luckier than before. This is what it said:

"Chief Yemelyanov, MUR. 'Admiral Nelson' left on the Moscow Express today in the international sleeping car. Possibly off on a serious tour. Paroled last year in accordance with the Amnesty. We had no reason to arrest him. Pre-revolutionary aliases: Jastrzębski, Romanescu, Schulz.

Chief of Odessa Investigation
Bureau, *Nikolayev*."

"What has this to do with dinars with holes in them?" I asked timidly.

"Quite a lot. I know 'Admiral Nelson' well. He's one of the best safe-crackers alive, one who began his career in tsarist times. They know him all over Europe. The last of the Mohicans, you might say. He's a king of the underworld and his word is law. He'll help us. Be here tomorrow morning, and we'll go to meet him at the station."

Next morning we were at the Kiev Station, waiting for the Odessa-Moscow Express.

When the train pulled in we approached the international sleeping car and waited for "Admiral Nelson." He appeared in a straw hat, a magnificent mackintosh on his arm, and carrying an impressive-looking cane with a large ivory lion's head knob. The "Admiral" was middle-aged, sparse, red-headed, with a single laughing and confident eye, the second being covered by a black silk eye-patch. He could have passed for a prosperous merchant, an old sea-wolf, a foreign concessionaire, or an international villain of the Russia Studios film series.

"Hello, 'Admiral'!" Osipov said. "Welcome to the capital!"

"Why, Osipov, what brings *you* here!" the "Admiral" exclaimed in delight and began shaking his hand so vigorously it would seem he had spent a sleepless night longing for this meeting. "Where have you been all this time? So the boys down at Investigation tipped you off about my arrival? Haven't they anything else to do, but bother a busy man? Ai-ai-ai. I've come as naked as a babe—no baggage, no instruments; so what are they squawking about? I'm here for a change of scenery, to look around and get back on my feet after the jug, but here they go annoying you! On the other hand, I'm grateful they did, because it gave me the chance to see you."

" 'Admiral,' I've a serious matter to discuss with you," Osipov interrupted. "Let's go some place where we can talk."

"As they used to say in Odessa, 'If the policeman says sit down, it isn't polite to stand,' " the "Admiral" said with a smile. "Let's go crack a bottle of beer and talk about life. And who's this nice young man?" he asked, pointing to me.

"He's a good friend of mine. He knows what it's all about."

Once in the restaurant, the "Admiral" listened to Osipov's story of the dinars with the holes and fell into a frenzy of indignation.

"What's going on in this capital of yours?" he fumed. "The Moscow burglars have degenerated, I tell you! What nerve—to break into a Commissar's apartment! Aren't there enough Nepmen for them, private offices and foreign concessions? But no, they go raising their hands against the Soviet Government! As a Soviet citizen, I say that this amounts to counter-revolution! Osipov, you know my *curriculum vitae* or whatever it's called, because I'm not too good at Latin. You know everything, and I'd like to ask you: did 'Admiral Nelson' ever touch a single government or even co-operative safe since the Great October Revolution? Yes, or no?"

"Not one, 'Admiral'!" Osipov agreed. "That's a fact."

"A fact? That's not a fact, it's a matter of world outlook and my *profession de foi*, as they say in French. Listen closely, young man, you're just starting out in life and it may be useful to you. My world outlook! Look at these hands of mine, which the Berlin Polizei-Präsident, at the World Congress of Criminologists in Vienna in 1913, called an outstanding phenomenon! Do you hear, that's just what he said: *'Meine lieben Herren, das ist wunderlich und artistisch.'* Now, have these hands ever hopped a single savings bank or even a rural branch of the State Bank? God forbid! I've always said to myself: 'Semyon, you better chop them off before you take a single penny from the people!' That's why I'm so angry!"

"Then what shall we decide, 'Admiral'?" Osipov asked, interrupting the indignant flow.

"Admiral Nelson" looked at him significantly and said in a quiet voice:

"You know my principles, don't you? In other words, you get the coins, not the man. Is that clear?"

"Quite," Osipov answered, ceremoniously rising as though to show that the High Contracting Parties had reached a solemn agreement.

Taking leave of the "Admiral," after he had jotted down Osipov's telephone number and promised to contact the necessary people immediately to "make a démarche and present an ultimatum," we got into our car and drove to MUR.

"Do you actually think this Odessa crook will be able to do anything?" I asked Osipov glumly.

"If the coins were stolen by a man, not a ghost, we'll have them in two days at most," he answered calmly. "You don't know him! The very fact that he has arrived in Moscow is already an event in the life of the underworld, and he's really mad. He'll raise the devil at the hide-outs! 'Admiral Nelson' never was and never will be an informer, I can vouch for that. But if you talk to him as man to man, he'll die rather than break his promise."

"He seemed an awful braggart to me," I said. "Take that story about the raptures of the Berlin Polizei-Präsident, for instance."

"Story?" Osipov snorted. "Let's go to my office and I'll show you what sort of a story that is. The man really has magic fingers."

Half an hour later I was leafing through the yellowed pages of a case-history of the Moscow Police Force; the inscription on the cover read:

"Jastrzębski, Kazimierz Stanislawovich, alias Jean Romanescu, alias Wilhelm Schulz, most dangerous international safe-cracker, working in the Empire and abroad; on the books of the police forces of St. Petersburg, Odessa, Moscow, Rostov-on-Don, Nakhichevan, and the Kingdom of Poland."

The case was stuffed with the reports and inquiries of these police forces, describing the adventures of the elusive "Admiral Nelson."

The most detailed of these was a memorandum by S. P. Beletsky, Chief of the Police Department of the Ministry of the Interior, addressed to His Excellency, N. A. Maklakov, Minister of the Interior, and dated March 12, 1913. In accordance with the Minister's resolution, copies of the memorandum were sent "for information and guidance" to the heads of the detective branches of the police forces of the largest cities in the Russian Empire.

The memorandum read as follows:

"Complying with the orders of Your Excellency, I present this report on the criminal activities of the well-known specialist in cracking and melting steel safes, a native of Odessa, known by the aliases of Jastrzębski, Romanescu and Schulz, who has had many previous convictions for the type of crime indicated above.

"This year, as in preceding years, the Police Department has been informed of the bold robberies of bank safes in various cities of the Empire. Especially noteworthy were the robberies committed in Nizhni-Novgorod and Samara.

"On the night of August 12, 1912, an unknown person made his way into the Nizhni-Novgorod branch of the Volga-Kama Bank where he opened two safes of a special design, ordered by the above-mentioned bank from the famous bank safe firm of Otto Grill & Company of Leipzig.

"As has been established at an inquiry conducted by members of the Nizhni-Novgorod detective force, aided by an official for special commissions attached to the Nizhni-Novgorod Governor's office, the criminal was in the bank no longer than thirty minutes, during which the night watchman, Ivan Kozolup, was absent from his post; the latter's long years of service in the bank and high recommendations from the local police station, the Nizhni-Novgorod Russian People's Union, and Father Varsonophy put him above suspicion.

"According to Kozolup, it was past 1 a. m. when he noticed that the traffic outside had ceased, the streets were deserted and the lights put out in the Rossiya Restaurant. He then decided to leave his post for a short time to have a cup of tea at home, as he was in the habit of doing to keep awake during the night, since he lived close by. He locked the entrance and started out. On the way he met a young man in a derby who asked him for a light.

"When Kozolup returned to his post after some thirty minutes, he found the outside door unlocked, as was the steel doors leading to the basement vaults. He immediately called the police and began looking for the bank's president Goloshchekin, Member of the City Duma, and an Honorary Citizen, who was not located until past 4 a. m., and then with difficulty and only with the aid of the local policeman, in a brothel in Kanavsky District run by Madame Skorokhodova.

"As was later established, the criminal had opened two safes with remarkable skill and an excellent knowledge of his trade, despite the fact that both had intricate secret locks. Taking nearly one hundred thousand rubles in bills from the safes, the criminal vanished in an unknown direction.

"Since the Leipzig firm of Otto Grill & Co. had issued a guarantee to the Board of the Volga-Kama Bank stating that its safes, due to the special and secret design of the locks, could never be opened by an uninstructed person, Mr. Goloshchekin immediately telegraphed the head of the firm, Herr Grill, and told him of the theft. The latter replied that very day that he was sending Herr Hans Schmeltz, the firm's senior engineer, to Nizhni-Novgorod, with all expenses paid. Several days later the above-mentioned Schmeltz arrived in Nizhni-Novgorod and, in the presence of the Bank President and the police officials, examined both safes with great care, after which he announced that he himself, the inventor of the secret locks and a specialist on safes, could never have opened them in thirty minutes, but would have required no less than five hours, and then only if he had had special tools.

"Then, in a private talk with the Nizhni-Novgorod Chief of Police, Schmeltz stated that should the criminal be found and duly punished, the firm of Otto Grill & Co. would gladly offer him a highly paid job after he had served his sentence. To corroborate his words, Schmeltz ventured to offer the Chief of Police a very expensive gift if the latter were to act as a middleman in negotiating with the criminal. Naturally, the Chief of Police refused the gift—at least he states as much in his report to the Nizhni-Novgorod Governor.

"Meanwhile, as the result of measures taken by the local police force, it was established that on August 13, an unknown, meticulously dressed red-headed young man in a derby bought a first-class ticket and boarded the *Princess Tatyana* on the Volga "Kavkaz & Merkuri" Steamship Co. which was to sail down the Volga. The same evening he joined in a card game with other passengers in the first-class salon. As later became known, the famous river-boat card-sharp, Zygmunt Przedecki, returning from the Nizhni-Novgorod Fair, where he had posed as the Polish Count Lankiewicz, and frequented large-stake games at the various gambling houses, was one of the players. Seeing that there were several Russian and Persian merchants on board returning from the fair, Przedecki started a game for high stakes in which the above-mentioned young man in a derby took part.

"According to the ship's steward, a Tatar named Murzayev, who served the players with refreshments and intoxicating drinks, the stakes were very high. They were playing for tens of thousands, and soon Przedecki had cleaned out the famous Samara flour merchant Prokhorov, two Persian merchants, Hussein Hajar and Suleiman Airom, as well as Count Kushelev, the Khvalynsk District Marshal of the Nobility. In all, he won no less than a hundred thousand rubles. According to Murzayev, the young man in the derby also lost a good deal. In paying the winner, he took the money from a large leather brief-case which, though he constantly kept it by his side, Murzayev noticed was stuffed with bills.

"After the game, when the passengers had retired to their cabins, Murzayev, who was cleaning the salon, heard a disturbance in the third cabin. Walking quickly to the door, he peeped through the keyhole. There he saw Przedecki and the young man in the derby. The latter was giving Przedecki a sound shaking: 'You crook!' he was shouting. 'Give me half your winnings, or I'll do you in,' to which

Przedecki yelled that he was willing to return only the money the young man had lost. They began to fight and the young man in the derby banged Przedecki on the head with a life-preserver until the gambler agreed to give up half of his winnings. Grabbing his small suitcase, Przedecki scrambled ashore at the first pier, despite the late hour. From the deck the red-headed man shouted gleefully after him: 'I'll show you Odessa-Mother, you tramp! You're a fop, not a card-sharp!' In general, he seemed very merry.

"Several days later, on the night after the *Princess Tatyana* had docked in Samara, where the man in the derby got off, an unknown criminal boldly robbed the Samara Merchants' Bank, where two safes were opened and one hundred and fifty-six thousand rubles stolen. Here, as in Nizhni-Novgorod, the job was done in a surprisingly short time.

"A police inquiry established that a red-headed young man in a derby entered the Volga Hotel on the evening the *Princess Tatyana* docked in Samara, presented a passport issued to Kazimierz Jastrzębski, and took a room. Close to three o'clock the next morning he returned from town carrying a suitcase and gave Agrafena Gorina, the chambermaid who opened the door for him, a five-ruble tip. When questioned, Gorina declared that he had been quite sober but obviously fatigued.

"These facts shed some light on the matter, since the famous safe-cracker Schulz-Romanescu was known to the Kharkov Police under the alias of Jastrzębski.

"But by the time these facts were received and checked, Schulz-Jastrzębski had disappeared.

"He was spotted in Berlin eight months later, when the Berlin Polizei-Präsidium reported the following event which caught the attention of the German police.

"In February of 1913 there was an industrial fair in Berlin at which German and other European firms exhibited their wares. In the 'Banking & Commercial Equipment' pavilion several firms displayed their new steel safes with secret locks, among them some made by Otto Grill & Co. One of the advertising devices used by this firm and the German Siemens-Schuckert electrical equipment firm, which displayed safes with secret electrical signalling mechanisms, was that both offered large rewards to any visitor who, firstly, could open a safe, and, secondly, could do so without touching off the alarm.

"On February 7, in the presence of a large crowd of visitors, a red-headed young man in a derby accosted the pavilion manager and said he would try to open a safe made by Otto Grill & Company of Leipzig and a Siemens-Schuckert safe as well. His offer was accepted and in twenty-two minutes he had opened both safes before the astonished representatives of the firm and the excited crowd; in the second case he had managed to switch off a secret alarm.

"He was handed the prize money on the spot, and in broken German invited all present to join him at the Wagner Beer Garden. After drinking a great deal, he did a tap dance and toasted the city of Odessa, calling it 'Odessa die Mutter.'

"Meanwhile, Hans Schmeltz, the afore-mentioned senior engineer of Otto Grill & Company, telephoned the Berlin police and said that the manner in which the stranger had opened the safe reminded him of something he had seen at the Nizhni-Novgorod branch of the Volga-Kama Bank.

"Representatives of the Berlin Polizei-Präsidium rushed to the Wagner Beer Garden and demanded the young man's passport. He showed them a Russian passport issued to one

Jastrzębski with an exit visa countersigned by the Konotop District police officer. The Berlin police officials, nevertheless, ordered him to come with them to establish his identity. Jastrzębski, however, flatly refused and sought protection from the crowd drinking at his expense. They rose to his defence to a man, and held the police officers, enabling him to make his getaway.

"In reporting the above to Your Excellency, I, on my part, consider it imperative to approach His Excellency, the Minister of Foreign Affairs, Sazonov, and ask him to appeal to the German police through the proper channels and demand that the above-mentioned Jastrzębski-Schulz be located, apprehended and extradited as a public enemy.

S. P. Beletsky, Chief of the Police
of the Ministry of the
Interior."

Further correspondence over the case showed that for nearly a year, the Ministry of the Interior, acting through the Ministry of Foreign Affairs, had been in contact with the German police, which searched for, or pretended to search for, "Admiral Nelson." This touching correspondence was interrupted by the war.

It was evening when I finished reading the yellowed documents, having copied several of the more interesting ones. Osipov and I set off for the Ars Cinema, where the Stanislavsky Dramatic Theatre now stands.

We bought two tickets and decided to have a walk, for we had nearly an hour till the film began.

"How do you think 'Admiral Nelson' will finish?" I asked Osipov.

"I often think of him and others like him," Osipov answered. "It's a difficult question, my friend. The past has left us a rather large underworld, with its own habits, traditions, differences and even 'schools' and professions. The years of the NEP have given them a fresh lease on life. The high-class restaurants, race tracks, privately-owned shops, private trade, cabarets and the Nepmen themselves all tend to foster crime. There are still many old-time 'specialists' at large—the burglars, thieves, proprietors of various dives, and so on. We'll catch most of them sooner or later and send them off to prison. Some will probably go straight and become honest citizens. It's hard to say just what the 'Admiral' will do. But it's a fact that he has never touched a penny of government or co-operative money in safes.

And that in itself is significant to my mind. Anyway, time will show."

The next morning began with a phone call from S.'s secretary who said her chief was still very upset and had asked her to remind us that there were only two days left. This didn't actually start me off in a bright mood. At two o'clock Osipov called to say "Admiral Nelson" had just phoned to say that the work was going full speed ahead, but that there were no coins in sight so far.

Towards the end of the day Sheverdin phoned, and I could tell by the anxiety with which this kind old man inquired about the case that he was really worried and thought I would be in for trouble if the coins were not found. I gave him a rough account of what the comrades at MUR were doing, but said that they had achieved nothing yet.

"That's too bad," he sighed. "Our victim is ready to blow his top. Do your best, my rosy-cheeked boy, do your best, or we'll really be in hot water."

One can imagine my excitement that evening when I heard the familiar siren of Osipov's car downstairs. I bolted out of the house and saw my friend's smiling face from afar;

beside him sat Nozhnitsky, one of his best assistants.

"Get in!" Osipov shouted. "The 'Admiral' called and asked us to meet him at the 'Cultural Corner' right away."

I got in and we raced down Gorky Street to a small house on the corner of Maly Gnezdnikovsky. The place has long been demolished and replaced by a large new house, but in those days it was the bar called the 'Cultural Corner,' famous not so much for its culture as for its excellent boiled crayfish, heavenly smoked herring and pickled green peas, all served with the beer.

"Admiral Nelson" was waiting for us at a table in a corner. Smartly dressed as always, he received us with a very solemn expression.

"Good evening!" he said with dignity. "You've certainly saddled me with a job, let me tell you! And I was hoping for a rest and a change of scenery! As my departed papa used to say: 'A rest like this may land you in a pine-box.' He was the keenest man in all Odessa, and there'll certainly never be another like him. By the way, he was the best fitter and mechanic in that great city; and my own experience shows that the laws of inheritance were not thought up by a bunch of crackpots.

I remember a time, and may I drop dead if it's not true...."

"Can't we get down to business?" Osipov interrupted. "You told me all about your departed papa back in 1921."

"Pardon me, I honestly forgot," the "Admiral" said. "Well, let's get down to business. Yesterday, straight from the station, I got the boys I wanted together and held a plenary meeting. I made such a speech that they all wept. 'You damned counter-revolutionary hydras,' I said. 'How could you dare to put the screws on a Commissar and grab a few stinky coins to shorten his valuable existence! Just because of some lousy dinars with holes you've been keeping a member of the government from important affairs of state. Rotters! I had to leave all my business in Odessa and dash up here only to say: *fooey*! They were spitting gall in the Moldavanka hide-out for three days when they heard what you'd done, you counter-revolutionaries! It's too low for words!' I spoke for at least half an hour, no less, and they had to give me three glasses of water, that's how excited I was. And then rose the king of the Moscow burglars—you know him," he turned to Osipov.

"Yes, I know, Senka Bars," Osipov nodded.

"Right. Shedding bitter tears, he swore it wasn't his work. Ah, what's the use of talking! The cream of Moscow was there! And they all swore to stop working until they found the damn coins that disgraced us all. And who should know better than you that they have really kept their word?"

"That's right," Osipov said. "For the first time in several years there wasn't a single burglary committed in the past twenty-four hours."

"Burglary?" the "Admiral" demanded, deeply hurt. "What do you mean burglary, when *no one* has lifted a finger these past twenty-four hours! We had to mobilize all the boys and everybody who was anybody. Was a single Nepman robbed, was a single doll relieved of her purse, was a single wallet missing? What's there to talk about, when the whole city's in a state of siege? Those dinars with holes are costing us a lot! Do you think any one of us has had so much as ten minutes' sleep? If you do, I'll stop respecting you."

"No, I don't think so," Osipov reassured him hastily.

"Because you're a smart man! More than that, I myself spent the night at the main hideout."

"In Zoologichesky Street?" Osipov asked with a smile.

"Didn't expect that from you," the "Admiral" said icily. "Never in his life has 'Admiral Nelson' put the finger on a single hide-out, and a question like that is out of order. I've nothing more to say."

"All right, forget it. Let's get on with that meeting."

"Fine. I stayed at the hide-out till morning, and they came running to me from all over the city every half hour, each saying: 'No!' By 7 a.m. there was not a doctor in the world who would have given a copper for my life, that's how beat I was. By eight I had one foot in the grave and could smell the dampness. My heart was barely beating and I had no pulse. Manka the Flea, the owner of the joint, just sobbed as she looked at me and wailed: 'My poor dear "Admiral," will you really die on me on account of some lousy dinars with holes? My God, what'll we tell them in Odessa? How will we ever explain why we couldn't save your life? They'll set my place on fire!' And who do you think saved me finally? Senka Bars. He came galloping in at 9:30. When he saw I was done for, he immediately hit on an idea. You see, he's a man with an exceptional educational background—he nearly graduated from a medical school in Zhmerinka, and God's my witness that if he hadn't become a burglar, he'd certainly have been a professor of medicine long since. Anyway, he dashed right off to the nearest hospital and there, in broad daylight, swiped an oxygen pillow from under some patient and brought it to me. God bless him, that was the only burglary committed that day. Not a bad rest I'm getting in Moscow, huh, Osipov?"

"Keep to the point, 'Admiral,'" Osipov insisted.

"We're getting to the heart of it now, and I'm about to drop anchor," the "Admiral" replied. "When I came to a bit, Kolya the Bunny, from Maryina Roshcha, broke in, looking as if he'd just wriggled off the Turkish Sultan's stake or stolen the British Crown Jewels in the 'B' tramway. He was yelling on top of his voice. 'What are you shouting about, idiot?' I asked. But he kept on until Senka Bars squeezed the dope out of him: the boys had found that lousy thief. First of all, he's not from Moscow. In the second place, which is much more important, he's not from Odessa, and, in the third, he's not even a real thief, but a visiting beginner from Tula. Now I ask you, how's a man to live in this crazy world?"

"Where are the coins?" Osipov asked calmly, looking the "Admiral" straight in the eyes.

"Not being a very original person, I asked Kolya the Bunny the same question," he answered caustically. "The coins are in Tula where the beginner shipped them. We've sent such a delegation after them that if as much as the famous arms factory is left standing in town, the city council can hold a special meeting of thanksgiving. They'll bring them back soon."

Even Osipov sighed with relief, and I grew dizzy with joy, while Nozhnitsky laughed till the tears streamed down his cheeks.

Just then someone tossed a pebble at the window, and "Admiral Nelson" jumped to his feet, shouting: "The ambassadors have arrived! Strike up the band!" With this, he hurled himself from the bar.

He returned a few minutes later with a look of triumph. He was carrying a rather large leather pouch with brass buckles.

"Here they are," he said, his only eye gleaming with satanic pride. "I'm willing to bet you anything that if all the police forces in the world, working hand-in-hand with the delegates of the Vienna International Congress of Criminologists, at which the Berlin Polizei-Präsident spoke so truthfully and warmly of my hands, were to gather here to search for these coins, they'd all drown themselves in the Moskva River for disgrace.... Young man," he said, turning to me, "you're just entering upon the road of life, and I've taken a great liking to you. Watch closely and remember what you see: and namely that thieves are capable of anything when their honour is at stake. That's 'Admiral Nelson' and his tremendous influence for you!"

He unbuckled the clasps and opened the pouch to reveal the coins nestling like doves in their special pockets.

We began to examine them. There were nearly two hundred and all were of copper, green and corroded with age; there were small coins and large ones, with bulls and serpents, eagles and rams, sphinxes and cranes.

"Let us rise to honour the Ages!" the "Admiral" said solemnly and actually rose. "Well, judging by the holes, these are the very same dinars that raised such a row. My God! What an ugly grimace of life, as Nikolai Shneyerzon, an Odessa barrister who defended me in 1915 when the police finally caught up with me, used to say. They're really awful. I hate to touch them. To think that the best people of this great city chased back and forth like a bunch of drunken cats—and all because of this trash. I can't see why the Commissar was so excited over this pile of rusty copper! True enough, great people, too, are fools sometimes, as the philosopher Spinoza used to say, though most probably he never said any such thing."

There was no stopping the "Admiral." He had had several shots of vodka and washed them down with a large beer, and now engulfed us with his eloquence. Courtesy would not let us interrupt him, since, after all, he had helped us. Osipov grew impatient, for he hated idle chatter. We were showered with philosophical platitudes and boastful reminiscences of an old safe-cracker, lyricisms and thieves' lore of the Moldavanka in Odessa.

When he finally ran dry, or, rather, wore himself out, we took advantage of a pause and were about to say good-bye, when he suddenly said:

"And do you know what the strangest thing about this strange case is? For the first time in his life 'Admiral Nelson' was on the side of the law. And I must say that being a detective is much more interesting! I give you my word as an old safe-cracker that these were the happiest twenty-four hours in my life."

The "Admiral" suddenly grew sober and gazed at us sadly, a middle-aged man who had unexpectedly realized that he had wasted his life.

Osipov sat up and looked at the "Admiral" keenly.

"This is the wisest and most important thing you've told us today, Semyon Mikhailovich," he said gravely, calling the "Admiral" by his real name for the first time. "And if, after having found these coins, you will also be able to find a new place for yourself in life, which is always possible if a man has a head and not a cabbage on his shoulders and a heart instead of a rotten egg, then you can count on me. I'd be glad to settle our account in this manner."

The "Admiral" blushed, and I understood that Osipov, as always, had struck home. Silence fell, the kind that is often more eloquent than any words.

The "Admiral" sat with bowed head, lost in thought.

Osipov's eyes never left him. They shone with the human sympathy which is as essential to the criminologist as faith in people if he is not to be narrow-minded and blind. Only too often in later years I came upon investigators who suffered from this blindness, and because of it, caused much unnecessary grief. After a long pause, the "Admiral" raised his head and said in nearly a whisper:

"I believe it was Archimedes who said: 'Give me a place to stand and I will move the earth.' I'm not Archimedes, and the world has moved without my help. But I can see that it has moved in the right direction, and that has moved something in me, too. I'm getting old, Osipov, and at my age it's difficult to begin life anew. But you had faith in me and that, too, is a place to stand, the sort Archimedes dreamed of. I will try to move my battered old world. I will try to melt the rusty safe I drag about inside of me. Who knows, perhaps there's something left there. Who knows?"

And rising suddenly, he ran off without even saying good-bye.

When I came to Sheverdin and told him what had happened, the old man laughed so loudly and long that he frightened me. Then, to my great surprise, he said very sternly:

"Nonetheless, my good fellow, I've consulted my colleagues and we've unanimously decided that you'll have to face the Disciplinary Collegium. That's how it is! So write an explanation."

I left Sheverdin's office in confusion and rushed to Snitovsky and Laskin, my tutors. Both were obviously out of sorts. Laskin barely mumbled a "hello," drumming the table, and Snitovsky was as cold as ice. M. Ostrogorsky, the assistant public procurator responsible for investigations, a tall handsome man with a bush of blond hair and large grey eyes which, at this moment, were very stern was also present.

"Small children—small worries, big children —big worries," Snitovsky began. "Comrade Sheinin (he had never addressed me that way before), I'm truly sorry, sorry about your strange behaviour. It's no good, my dear sir, it's no good. I would even venture to say—it's a shame! Is that what we have taught you, sir?"

"But permit me. . ." I mumbled.

"No, I won't!" Snitovsky interrupted, banging the table. "I won't! To think that a court investigator should be sitting in a bar with a professional criminal! It's terrible! Terrible!"

"It's unheard of!" Laskin stormed.

"I just can't understand it," Ostrogorsky muttered.

"When Sheverdin told us what happened, we felt we shouldn't let it pass lightly. This will be a lesson to you. Yes, a lesson not to besmirch our profession."

A week later I stood before a large table covered with a heavy green cloth and faced a plenary Disciplinary Collegium of the Regional Court with gloomy, bearded Degtyaryov in the chair.

By that time my dear tutors had completely convinced me that I had committed a great and unpardonable sin. And I told our Collegium most sincerely what had happened, how and why. And oh, how wretched I was!

Degtyaryov listened attentively to every word and, strange as it may seem, somewhere in the depths of his brown ominous eyes there was a kind, and I would even say merry, twinkle. Perhaps that was why he chewed his beard so fiercely, growling from time to time:

"Out with it! Out with it all! Tricky, aren't you! So you wanted to be another Sherlock Holmes!"

All this came back to me later. At the time, however, I was in no position to analyze anything and was only afraid to omit something in my nervousness. I told them all there was to tell.

The judges conferred a short twenty minutes, but it seemed an eternity to me. And when Degtyaryov read their verdict it was with great difficulty and through a fog that I grasped the main point: I was not to be kicked out. In view of my youth and sincere repentance, the Collegium had decided to let the matter with a severe rebuke. All this happened very long ago and I may as well confess that I burst into tears. To this Degtyaryov responded in a very kindly and unfamiliar tone, saying softly:

"That's all right. No need to be ashamed. Cry as much as you like, and I hope this will be the least of your misfortunes."

I met "Admiral Nelson" again many years later, in the thirties. I was then working in the Procurator's Office of the U.S.S.R. as Chief of the Investigating Bureau. One day, entering the office of I. Akulov, Chief Procurator of the U.S.S.R., I found him extremely upset.

"Just see what's happened," he said. "I've lost the key to my safe and I'm due to report to the Government in two hours, but all my papers are in there. Our locksmith won't touch it, because it's a special safe with a secret lock. He says it will take a day of hard work to open it."

I looked at the massive safe, and then I remembered that Osipov several years before had told me that "Admiral Nelson" had severed his ties with his past. He had moved to Moscow and was working diligently as a chief mechanic in a metal-working co-operative.

"Wait a minute," I said. "I think I can help you."

I immediately phoned Osipov and told him what had happened.

"Say no more, old man. I'll try to find Semyon Mikhailovich for you. If I succeed I'll come along with him. But I haven't seen him for nearly a year, and I don't even know if he's still alive."

"Isn't that the 'Admiral Nelson' you told me about?" said Akulov, who understood everything at a hint, the moment I laid down the receiver.

"Yes."

"Well, judging from the past, he's the man for the job. The old-timers never let us down, do they?"

And he smiled in his own peculiar way, the soft, sly smile his colleagues knew so well.

In less than half an hour Osipov arrived, a bit short winded, but still strong. He was followed by a neatly dressed old man carrying a small suitcase. The man had one eye, the other being covered by a small black eye patch. The years had done their work. It was difficult to recognize the "Admiral," he had aged so in the interval. Yet somewhere deep in his only eye there glowed the spark I remembered from our first encounter.

Akulov greeted the "Admiral," saying:

"How do you do? Won't you please sit down? I was told you were one of the best ... uh ... mechanics. Is that so?"

"There was a time when every police force in Europe thought so," the "Admiral" replied with dignity. "The police, it's true, make mistakes more often than anyone else. Still, I did know a bit about safes. Is this the one?" He pointed to the ill-fated safe.

"That's right. If I'm not mistaken, it's a German one."

"Yes, it's a Leipzig safe," the "Admiral" agreed examining it. "But it's not a 'prima,' as the Germans say. It's an Otto Grill & Company safe. I've handled them before. What we have here is a double lock of stainless steel with an inner-spring and an automatic side brake—over here on the left—which holds back the lock, *if* you don't know the secret. And here's the secret itself. It's a musical one. Can't be helped, the Germans like music."

And "Admiral Nelson" pressed the head of one of the five brass bolts which held the lock in place. It immediately gave way and moved aside with a pleasant ring.

"That's right," Akulov agreed. "I see the police were not always wrong, Semyon Mikhailovich—if I'm not mistaken? You really are an expert."

"Don't praise me beforehand, or you'll jinx it," the "Admiral" answered. "Now this 'German' and I will really get to know each other."

The "Admiral" then pulled from his suitcase a thin steel rod and a long key with a movable bit which he began manipulating noiselessly.

"Safe locks can't stand rough handling," he said as he worked. "One must be gentle with them. They're just like women, and prefer gentleness to brute strength. It may sound funny to hear an old wreck like me speaking of women, but in his youth the former 'Admiral Nelson' knew other things besides safes, even if he had only one eye. By the way, Comrade

Akulov, that's how I got my nickname. Admiral Nelson also had one eye. In 1905 I was touring Amsterdam and, since bygones are bygones anyway, I might as well tell you that I touched a very good safe. The next day I read a story in the papers saying that in a week England was going to commemorate the 100th anniversary of the death of Horatio Nelson. As you know, he was killed on October 21 in the battle of Trafalgar, when he defeated the Franco-Spanish fleet. I wanted to do my bit for my namesake, and bought a lot of the famous Dutch tulips in Amsterdam, loaded them on a ship and sailed for England. Three trucks took my tulips to the cemetery. I myself wore a new frock coat and top hat for the occasion. Upon my word, when the public saw my tulips they were more interested in me than in the First Lord of the Admiralty. And then I delivered a speech. 'Ladies and Gentlemen,' I said. 'It's an honour and a pleasure to represent the inimitable city of Odessa, which has given the world so many outstanding poets, musicians, sailors and criminals. Your one-eyed Admiral knew his business, a quality which, by the way, is characteristic of many one-eyed people.' My words were met with an ovation. Yes, as Kant said: 'In our old age we have only our memories,' though I'm not really sure of that."

"That only memories remain, or that those were Kant's words?" Akulov asked quickly.

"Comrade Osipov can confirm that we are now speaking only of Kant, and the fact that I've had nothing but memories to fall back on for many a year is something the entire Criminal Department is positive of, not only myself."

"That's true," Osipov agreed.

At that moment the "Admiral" said: "Thanks a lot, dearie," and opened the safe.

Akulov thanked him and tactfully asked how much he owed him, but the "Admiral" was so indignant, the matter was dropped at once.

"Thanks again, Semyon Mikhailovich," Akulov said. "I'm really glad I met you *now*, when you've already passed a difficult and perhaps the most difficult test in life. And I'm not speaking about the safe."

"I understand you, Comrade Akulov," the "Admiral" answered softly. "You're thinking of the man who opened it. To be frank, I began preparing for this test long ago, at the time we were looking for the dinars with holes. Now I visit the Pushkin Museum every year. They have a department of ancient coins there, and I look at those dinars and thank the unknown and long-since departed craftsmen who cast them so many years ago. But I'm still more thankful to the living and known craftsmen who are casting our wonderful times and are even re-casting such rubbed-out coins as me. May our times and our people thrive for ever, Comrade Procurator!"

"I'd like to shake hands with you!" Akulov said, seemingly not quite to the point, but actually in response to the "Admiral's" words.

1956

THE WOLF PACK

Early in 1928, when I was transferred to Leningrad, there was quite a crime wave in the city and the Leningrad investigators were swamped with cases. The NEP was flourishing, differing from the Moscow version in the Nepmen themselves, most of whom were representatives of the pre-revolutionary commercial élite and closely connected with the remnants of the former capital's aristocracy. The Leningrad Nepmen were only too happy to marry into the families of princes and counts and copied the old Petersburg "high society" in their way of life and manner.

The Nepmen not infrequently swindled the representatives of the government concerns and enterprises with whom they signed all sorts of agreements and contracts. Aiming to corrupt the Soviet workers they met, the Nepmen tried to arouse in them a desire for an "easy life" by means of bribes and various small favours, treats and "presents." There were many temptations. In the famous Vladimir Club, located in a magnificent mansion with columns along the façade at Nakhimson Prospekt, there was a fashionable casino with sleek croupiers in dress suits and expensive call girls. The famous pre-revolutionary restaurateur Fyodorov, a giant with a face like a prize pumpkin, re-opened his restaurant and amazed his *gourmet clientèle*. His competitors were the owners of Sans-Souci, Italia, the Elephant, Palermo, Quisisana, Oblivion and Delight.

The famous bar in the cellar of the European Hotel did a thriving, noisy business until dawn; it had a three-storey hall, three orchestras, a sea of tables at which souteneurs and prostitutes, artists and Nepmen, pick-pockets and robbers, former princes and princesses, ruddy-cheeked sailors and students sat and drank, ate and sang, laughed, argued and made love.

Pretty flirtatious flower girls, who sold more than their violets, and waiters in white moved among the tables, dazed by the noise, the music, the faces and the flashy clothes.

The kings of the Leningrad NEP—the Kühns,

Magids, Simanovs, Salmans, Krafts and Fyo-
dorovs—usually caroused in the best restaurants: The First Society in Sadovaya Street,
Fyodorov's, Astoria, or on the Roof Garden of
the European Hotel. The railway station restaurant of the Sestroretsk Spa, which had a
huge open terrace facing on the sea and featured the newly popular jazz was a summer
favourite. People came here by car at night
after a premier at Utyosov's Free Theatre, the
Music Hall, or the Theatre of Comedy, sub-
leased as a private enterprise by Nadezhdin
and Granovskaya, a very talented comedy
team and the toast of the town.

Here, at exquisitely served tables on the
cool, softly lit terrace, to the quiet sounds of
the waves lapping at the dark shore, the
"kings" made deals involving millions; they
haggled, formed commercial alliances, drew up
agreements, and in great detail discussed the
"general situation," which they considered
tense and unpromising in 1928.

The most far-sighted began to understand
that the "temporary retreat" was coming to an
end and that the young but already sturdy
state industry, commerce and co-operatives
were beginning to advance on the private sec-
tor. The Nepmen were especially worried by

the taxes on their profits and spared no breath in cursing Sergei Ter-Avanesov, the Chief of the Taxation Department of the Leningrad Regional Financial Department; he was in charge of the revenue inspectors and was known to be "unapproachable."

True, towards the end of 1927 a little rumour made the rounds that the paint manufacturer Kühn and the chocolate manufacturer Kraft had, in some mysterious way, been able to find their way into Ter-Avanesov's good graces. However, when questioned by their own friends among the other "kings," they denied this so warmly and sincerely that, in the end, they were believed.

Then, suddenly, a series of ominous events took place at the beginning of 1928: in a single day Ter-Avanesov, over a dozen revenue inspectors and many important Nepmen, including Kraft, Salman, Magid, Fyodorov and many others, were arrested. Rumour had it that the investigating offices had discovered many instances in which the revenue inspectors had accepted bribes from the Nepmen for lowering their taxes. The famous Kühn vanished into thin air; his paint factory was attached by the authorities. Yanaki, a Greek from Odessa, who alone controlled nearly the whole of the antique furniture market, disappeared on the same night as Kühn. The old revenue inspectors were replaced, and it was absolutely impossible to approach the new men.

The *Evening Red Gazette*, which had a very large circulation because it was running a sensational serial entitled *The Diary of Lady-in-Waiting*, the memoirs of Vyrubova, the Empress's favourite and Rasputin's mistress, printed a rather mysterious but ominous article which stated that the case of the revenue inspectors who had unlawfully slashed the taxes of the Nepmen was developing successfully and that new suspects had been uncovered. The nightly trips to Sestroretsk and the carousing at the Astoria and the Roof Garden stopped. Many private shops and societies began to close down. Cabs and automobiles with yellow circles on the doors to indicate that the vehicle was for hire stood idle at the cab stands, for passengers became a rarity.

The "front line" of the NEP had obviously been broken in many places.

The important group case of the revenue inspectors and the Nepmen, receivers and givers of bribes, was forwarded to me. This case ran into many volumes recording dozens of episodes, thousands of documents and numerous opinions by expert commissions. The job was an extremely strenuous one and the regional procurator in charge of the case kept hurrying us, as it was constantly in the public eye.

There is a widespread and false opinion that the investigator dealing with the so-called economic and official cases rarely comes in contact with human drama, psychological conflicts and strong emotions. This is not so. In such common crimes as jealousy murder, suicides, corruption, etc., the "theme" of the case itself brings the investigator face to face with psychological problems of love, jealousy, revenge, cunning, deceit, compulsion, etc. In such cases it is impossible to complete an investigation without a clear picture of these problems, all of which are of paramount importance, if only because they throw light on the *motives* of the crime, on the reasons and circumstances which prompted its conception and perpetration.

In a case of bribery, it is true, these questions may not arise at all, but the court, after first establishing the fact of a bribe having been offered and received, must then determine the reason *why* this was done. As in any other criminal case, this cannot be limited to confessions from the two sides, for an investigator's sole reliance on a confession as the "king of all proofs" either shows his ineptness in legal and psychological matters, or his unwillingness or inability to handle his job properly. In the case of the revenue inspectors and the Nepmen, practically all the defendants had confessed, but these confessions had to be checked and corroborated by documents and figures, as this was a case of illegal tax reduction.

That is why I considered it my duty to establish the fact of the illegal tax cut and its exact amount for a given bribe in every one of the many instances of the case.

On the other hand, I was no less concerned with a problem that, I was convinced, had both social and psychological importance, namely, how it could have come about that a large group of people, Communists among them, who had been placed in key positions in the financial battle, could have committed what amounted to treason, acting as turncoats in some cases, as enemy agents in others. I tried to find the answer in the life story and character of each of the revenue inspectors involved. And gradually, this side of the case began to clear up. The reasons behind their actions for the most part were drunkenness and moral instability, unavoidable depravation due to lack of will and principles, greed, the desire for easy money and the systematic, shrewd entanglement of them by the Nepmen. One came to take bribes because he had never had any sincere beliefs, definite views or faith in the cause he was serving. Another started drinking, becoming an alcoholic who had drunk away his honour and his future before he knew it. A third, who had always been an honest man, fell into bad company and, from the small favours and presents he accepted from the Nepmen shrewd enough to approach him, evolved into a die-hard bribe taker who had completely succumbed to the old formula: "Ah, to hell with everything!" A fourth, having been taken firmly in tow by an avaricious wife ever nagging that everyone else was doing so well, while she, poor thing, could not even buy herself a fur coat, finally accepted the coat from a tax-payer and found himself in his claws.

I particularly remember one curious episode. A Nepman named Girs, a very sharp and cunning man, managed to induce a revenue inspector named Platonov to accept a seal-skin coat for his young, pretty and very demanding wife whom he adored. After this, the Nepman proceeded to tie Platonov into knots beginning to receive bribes from other Nepmen in the inspector's name, keeping the lion's share for himself and making his victim obey him in everything. Platonov, a young, blue-eyed, blond-haired man with a kind face and the full, soft lips of a weak-willed sensuous person attempted to rebel several times, but Girs, already sure that he had him safely under his heel, would meaningly raise an eyebrow and repeat the same phrase in his rasping voice: "My dear man, I think you're beginning to forget how indebted you are to me." This was said in so threatening a tone accompanied by such a vicious, icy stare, that Platonov was immediately quelled and begging pardon, though deep in his heart he cursed this devil, his pretty wife and the wretched seal-skin coat that had made him a slave.

Then, as in my later years as an investigator, I found many instances of weak-willed, unstable people, who were formerly blameless, but came to be completely dominated by another's evil and criminal will. I was always sorry for such unfortunates, despicable though they were for the dumb and animal-like submissiveness which had turned them into slaves. The weak will is the sister of crime, and I was often witness to this terrible relationship!

The Trap

While working on this case I came upon a striking example where love and lack of will-power turned a previously honest man into a dangerous criminal, wrecking his formerly un-spotted life. Sergei Ter-Avanesov was the man in question.

He had worked in the Leningrad Regional Revenue Office from the early days of the Rev-olution. He was an economist, undoubtedly a great financial expert and a good worker. Though not a Party member, he, according to the then accepted phrase, "fully supported the platform of the Soviet Government."

Ter-Avanesov was no longer young and a bachelor. First his studies, and then the rush of work had taken all his time, until, on his fiftieth birthday, he discovered that his life was nearly over, that he had never had a fam-ily and children, nor even a serious love affair.

"I looked at myself in the mirror very closely that day to see myself as others saw me," he said to me. "I didn't like the small, round middle-aged man with a large bald spot and a puffy face who was looking glumly back at me and seemed to be saying: 'Oh, brother, see what you've done to me! You're old, you're an old man and you have nothing to remember in your old age. A financial book-worm! What did you ever see, you idiot, but the paragraphs and articles of the budget, and extra charges and assessments? Did you ever have a real love affair with a real woman, a love affair that made your heart throb, that robbed you of sleep, that tortured you with jealousy, making you wander along the Neva embankments on the white nights, that drove you desperate because she was indifferent or ecstatic when she finally said *yes?*' In general, it was a terrible day with a most unhappy summing up of most unhappy conclusions."

Ter-Avanesov sighed and lit a cigarette. My windows which opened on the Fontanka let in the noise of a sunny May day. Off in the distance lay the green Summer Garden, with children's voices ringing merrily in the air.

"This actually has nothing to do with my case," Ter-Avanesov said suddenly. "I have confessed accepting bribes from Kühn and Kraft as payment for lowering their taxes. All the rest is just words, something to think about in my cell."

"But did you ever accept any bribes before?"

"Never! I had nothing to be ashamed of until the autumn of 1927! My word of honour!"

This was said with such warmth and conviction that I could not help believing him. Besides, there was nothing to show that Ter-Avanesov had taken a single wrong step in all his long years of service in the Financial Department. On the contrary, his attitude towards his official duties had been common knowledge and above reproach.

What could have pushed this well-educated, formerly honest and completely mature person from the path he had followed so steadily for so many years?

He was the only one who could have answered that question, but apparently had no desire to do so. Several times, after questioning him, I tried to channel the conversation along this vein, explaining that I was not interested in it "for the record"; but he would only smile sadly and tactfully though firmly avoid answering.

Meanwhile, the investigation of the case was coming to an end. The defendants' wives were allowed weekly visits and each Thursday these women would come to me for their passes. Ter-Avanesov's wife was one of them. He had married her two years before. She was a very attractive young woman with large greenish eyes, a delicately up-tilted nose and full, capricious lips. She, like the other wives, inquired gravely about her husband's health, received her pass and, nodding her pretty head, disappeared. I noticed that she always came with a young and elegant blond man of about her own age who waited for her in the corridor. Each time they would leave together. Once or twice as I looked through the window, I noticed them strolling down the Fontanka Embankment arm-in-arm, she laughing at something he was saying. She usually brought a linen-covered package with provisions which she would leave with an attendant to be given to her husband. I noticed that the writing on the packages was always in blue indelible pencil and in a confident, firm and professional hand.

"Who does that wonderful lettering on your packages?" I once asked her when she entered my office carrying a small food parcel.

"A friend of ours does it," she said, colouring slightly.

"The one who usually accompanies you?"

"Yes," she answered reluctantly.

I did not question her further, especially as it had no bearing on the case, but thought to myself that Ter-Avanesov was paying dearly for having married a woman twenty-five years younger than himself. This situation, grave in itself, was aggravated by the fact that the woman's husband was in jail and that she knew that the least he could count on would be ten years in a work camp.

As an investigator I had unfortunately often seen that the wives of the defendants rarely remained true to them. Even in the initial stages of the investigation, these young women would sometimes cast about anxiously for an "emergency landing," as one of them once put it quite frankly and cynically.

The wife of Platonov, who went under because of a seal-skin coat was a full-bosomed, stately young woman with brown hair; she used perfume freely, had a stylish hair-do and a flirtatious manner. After she had missed two successive visiting days, and I received a frantic note from Platonov, I summoned her and asked why she had not come or sent anything to her husband.

"Can't he understand," she answered, calmly turning her large beautiful grey eyes on me, "that I have to think about myself, too? After all, I can't be the wife of a jail-bird and sit crying over my broken life! I'm no child, I'm twenty-eight, and it's not easy to find a good husband. Thank God, I have no children, because I'd really have a hard time getting married if I did."

"Do you think you have no responsibilities to your husband, and isn't it partly your fault that he is here?" I asked, unable to control myself.

"Now don't say that it was my fault! It's simply that he's a dunce and wasn't smart enough. As for responsibilities, there's a limit to everything. I gave him all I had—my youth, my beauty, and my first love, and it was up to him to make my life beautiful. He wasn't able to, and that's just too bad for him."

Once more I was up against the finished philosophy of a certain category of women who consider getting married as a step upward in the world, and think their husbands are obliged to provide them with a comfortable living as a sort of payment for their "youth, beauty and first love." I still cannot understand why it never occurs to these ladies that their husbands, too, give them their youth, and often their first love. Why, then, are the "investments" of one side only to be quoted, and not of the other?

It must be said for the sake of justice that there were still predatory men occasionally who fell upon young and beautiful women whose husbands were in jail like wolves on sheep. They apparently thought that finding herself in difficult straits, the wife of an arrested man would be more "reasonable." Such a scoundrel would shower her with that peculiarly studied "attention," always important to a woman, and especially to one in such a situation, and in the end have his way. If the woman held a job or had some savings, the parasite would try to gain more than love's favours from her.

The blond, light-eyed, elegant young man who accompanied Ter-Avanesov's wife when she came for her visitor's pass was just such a sharper as this. I had noticed him from the start, but was not aware of the role he had played in the life of this family until the day Ter-Avanesov was told that the investigation was over. After he signed a paper stating that he had been acquainted with the documents of the case and had nothing to add, he suddenly said:

"You've asked me several times how with my background, outlook on life and beliefs I came to be a bribe taker, and I've always avoided answering you. But this is the last time we're sitting here together. Next come the trial and my sentence. Before we part, I'd like to thank you for your humane attitude, something no one could appreciate better than a man in my position. And then I'd like to tell you how Ter-Avanesov became a criminal. Will you allow me?"

"Certainly. I've always wanted to know."

"Well, then, listen. I've decided to tell you everything now that the investigation is over and what I say will not go into the record, because it's *not* for the record."

"Six months after my fiftieth birthday—remember, I began telling you about it once?—I had to stay late at the office one evening to dictate an urgent report to Moscow. It was at the end of May, when the white nights begin in Leningrad. I must say, by the way, that I never shared the general poetic ecstasy over those nights. That unprincipled mixture of day

and night, that illusory twilight enveloping
the sleeping city and interfering with everyone's sleep, that pale, sickly sun rising slowly
from a sicklier dawn all went against my grain
and interfered with my work. I'm sure science
will some day discover something unhealthy
and noxious about those white nights; anyway it's not surprising that all my troubles began on a white night. In a word, I had to dictate an urgent report, and since all the typists
in my department had already left, I called for
the typist on duty. Some minutes later a very
pretty young girl came in. The porter brought
her typewriter, and I began to dictate."

Ter-Avanesov interrupted his story to light
a cigarette. He struck one match after another, but his hands shook and the flame went
out each time before he could light up. He
was obviously upset and trying not to show
it; that was why I did not offer him a light,
pretending that his unsuccessful attempts were
quite natural.

"Your matches are damp," I finally said.
"Would you like to try mine?"

I lit a match. He inhaled deeply several
times, then turned to me abruptly, saying:

"To make a long story short, I married the
girl two months later. I was very happy, but

always busy at work, coming home late so that my wife, naturally, was lonely. The wife of a high official is not to be envied. To tell you the truth, I still can't understand who thought up these midnight sessions, endless conferences and late summonses to the chiefs. But that's not the point. Galya began to feel lonely. I would come home late and tired, grab a bite to eat and fall into bed like a log. Once, after a long conversation, she said quite frankly that she was tired of such a life. I suggested that she find some friends and go to theatres without me. I had no other choice. Then, one day she introduced me to a young man whom she had met at her girl-friend's house. He was an artist, but apparently not a very talented one, because he worked in a Leningrad advertising office where he hardly did any drawing himself. He was in charge of the orders and book-keeping there. But he seemed quite content with his life. Soon he became a daily visitor at our house. I would come home and always find Georgi there. He was tactful, polite though, unfortunately, a bit too sugary. His sensuous eyes were a transparent blue and his nose was a bit too long. It seemed to be prying into things. Frankly, I found him repulsive. He was a fop with a high-flown

103

manner, a barber's elegance and a degenerate's rotten teeth. Always fawning, he affected an exalted tone when speaking of the "sacred art" which he supposedly served. I sensed that the bounder had a bit of the pimp in him, but for many reasons said nothing to my wife, never dreaming she could be unfaithful. Such a thing never occurred to me!"

It was quite late when Ter-Avanesov finished his story. I was amazed, but did not yet know that this story of astounding human baseness involved a trap, cunningly contrived for him by the Nepmen. He himself was still less in a position to realize this, knowing only what he had told me.

Six months after Ter-Avanesov's wife had begun seeing Georgi, he came to her in tears and delivered himself of a tragic monologue, saying that he had come "to say farewell for ever," as he had lost ten thousand rubles of government funds at the Vladimir Club, that he "could not stand the disgrace" and had decided to commit suicide.

When Ter-Avanesov came home from work late that night he found his wife sobbing bitterly. It took him a long time to comfort her.

Finally, she told him that she loved Georgi and could not bear his misfortune. Ter-Avanesov was shaken by two simultaneous blows: the news that his wife had been unfaithful and her threat to commit suicide if her lover were not saved.

"Now I realize that Galya's threat of committing suicide on that terrible night weakened my reaction to the disclosure that she had been unfaithful," Ter-Avanesov said. "Strange as it may seem, it would have been much worse if I had discovered only that she had been unfaithful. When she told me so definitely that she would kill herself if I didn't save Georgi, I understood how terribly dear this woman was to me."

Ter-Avanesov rose, walked about the room and, returning to the desk at which I sat, continued:

"She was so grief-stricken and sobbed so, begging me to save the man she sincerely loved, the one without whom she could not live, that I finally promised I'd get the money at any cost. But where could I have got it? My small savings melted away at an amazing rate after my marriage. Our expenses had been great and I never wanted to deny Galya anything. The most I could get at work was an advance of a month's salary. I had no friend from whom to borrow such a sum. And then, the very next day, when I was racking my brains to find a way to get that damn money, the paint manufacturer Kühn, one of the big Leningrad Nepmen, came to complain about his taxes. The devil immediately noticed that I was upset. Like the rest of them, he had known me for many years. He asked what was wrong and I said I was tired, but he understood that something unusual had happened. Then, for the first time in my life, a terrible thought occurred to me: here was a man who would be glad to give me the ten thousand rubles on the spot and without any special pleading on my part, and no one in the world except us two would ever know of it, since he would want it to be secret as much as I. And this damn German–Kühn comes from the Baltic Germans–just wouldn't leave. He seemed to have sensed that I was in trouble. Trouble that he could put to his own use.

"I'm twice your age, but you're a senior investigator and question criminals every day. Can you tell me how, why and in what way these vultures sense that you've turned into carrion? Yes, carrion; that's exactly what I became that day! What were the invisible signs

that told these Kühns and Krafts, Simanovs
and Salmans that 'Ter, who could not be
bought'—that's what they used to say about
me—had suddenly become 'willing'? I didn't
have to ask Kühn for the money. He offered
it to me himself that day. I was burning up
with shame and a feeling of my own foulness
as I sold myself to him like a trollop from
Nevsky Prospekt!

"When I came home late that night and gave
my wife the money she wept with joy, embraced me and said she would never forget what
I had done. And then, worried, that her Georgi
would be unable to stand the suspense, she
dressed and took him the money. I swear, that
was the most dreadful night in my life, more
awful than my first night in jail!

"Naturally, I swore to myself that I'd do
everything possible to pay Kühn back—I'd
economize, work overtime and sell my belongings. But still, I had to cut his taxes.

"Then, exactly a month later, I again found
my wife in hysterics. Georgi had apparently
decided to win back his money and had instead lost fifteen thousand more. He again told
Galya he'd commit suicide and she again
pleaded with him. Again she screamed and
said that if I didn't get the money and Georgi

died, she'd drown herself in the Neva. And again I promised I would.

"I phoned Kühn myself. He came immediately and I babbled something about the possibility of his lending me another fifteen thousand. He looked at me in surprise and said he considered "our previous account settled," but was ready to help me. I was overjoyed. Then I discovered his help meant he intended to ask his friend Kraft to give me the money. An hour later he returned with Kraft and re-sold me to him like a ram. Then again my wife kissed me and swore she would never forget what I had done, and again she dashed off to her darling Georgi with the money. She returned the next morning and was calm, happy and content."

Ter-Avanesov lit another cigarette. The lights went on on the Fontanka Embankment. We could hear the laughter and shouting of young people rowing on the river and the sounds of a band playing on Mars Field.

I phoned for a guard to take him back to prison.

In parting, he said softly:

"I have a last request to make: don't allow my wife to send me any packages. Every time I get one with that 'artistic' handwriting I go mad! Doesn't that louse realize how disgusting and terrible it is for me? That's my only request."

After what Ter-Avanesov had told me, I wanted to find the lost Kühn more than ever. I knew that he had two families: his old wife, whom he did not want to abandon, and a second one, rather a mistress, a young and beautiful brunette named Maria Fyodorovna. It was discovered that this young woman occupied a luxurious apartment in an aristocratic mansion on the Palace Embankment. She never lacked money and continued to live extravagantly despite Kühn's sudden disappearance. She had not tried to find work and was apparently still in contact with the Nepman.

Summoned to my office, she stated calmly and emphatically that she "had no idea" where Kühn might be, had received no letters from him, and could be of no help in the matter.

She was an olive-skinned, dark-eyed elegant woman, very self-possessed. It was only too clear that she would say nothing. But talking to her, I learned she was friendly with the wife of another defendant in the case, a young woman much less attractive than she.

Though still a young investigator, I knew that if such women were friends, the less attractive of the two would probably hate the other deep down in her heart and envy her awfully. I recalled a little thing that had happened before I was transferred to Leningrad. In one of my cases I had occasion to question an elderly woman who had owned a millinery shop in fashionable Stoleshnikov Street for many years. When asked about the friendship of two women acquaintances, she smiled sarcastically, puffed at her cigarette and drawled:

"Comrade Inspector, I've been selling hats for thirty years. It has never happened that a woman came in to buy a hat without her friend, and it has also never happened that her girl-friend gave her the right advice. That's all I have to say about two women being friends."

The old milliner's original parable, I am sorry to say, often fitted the case when I had to look into the so-called friendship of women. True, it is only just that I should add that as a criminologist I usually came up against women of a specific circle and background and, therefore, with a definite psychological outlook.

Both Maria Fyodorovna and her friend belonged to this category, and that was why I decided to mention Maria Fyodorovna to the other when she came to my office as usual on a Thursday for her visitor's pass. She glanced up at me quickly. A doubtful shadow crossed her face, and she began to speak in a whisper:

"Ah, what's she got to worry about! She's living on the fat of the land! She's become so brazen, she's even sent for her Kühn. Just this morning she said to me: 'I feel like I'm on my honeymoon.'"

Half an hour later, having procured a search warrant, I drove up to the mansion in which Maria Fyodorovna lived. I was accompanied by the Regional Court commandant and his assistant. Making sure that there was no back stairway, we rang at the front door. After a long while we heard light steps behind the massive door and a young maid in a pretty apron let us in. When I asked if her mistress was home, she said yes. Just then Maria Fyodorovna, in a dressing gown, entered the anteroom. I presented her with the warrant and explained that the search was to "discover the whereabouts of one Nikolai Kühn, at present a fugitive from justice." She heard me out very calmly, smiled and said:

"Why, please come in! My house is at your disposal! Kühn isn't here and I don't know where he is. It's a pity you don't trust women, Comrade Inspector."

It was a modern, exquisitely furnished seven-room apartment. Unlike the usual Nepmen's homes of the time—expensively furnished with extremely bad taste—Maria Fyodorovna's house was furnished with great care and good taste. We searched room after room, beginning with the anteroom. There was not a sign of Kühn anywhere, and, to tell the truth, I was ready to believe that Maria Fyodorovna's friend had lied to me. We finally reached the last room—the bedroom. I noticed that the low, wide bed of magnificent Karelian birch and bronze was undone, that both pillows were dented, and that a man's pocket-watch lay ticking nonchalantly on the night table. I looked at Maria Fyodorovna's wrist and saw that she was wearing her watch. In an ashtray on the night table were several cigarette butts chewed at the tips like men have the habit of doing.

When Maria Fyodorovna caught me looking at the butts she immediately pulled a Sappho from a pack and lit it. I was determined to have the last word in this display and waited for her to finish the cigarette. When she did I asked her for the butt. She handed it to me in surprise. Naturally, the end was not chewed at all. I showed it to her and compared it with one from the ash-tray, one which had been smoked by a man.

"As you see, Maria Fyodorovna, these cigarettes were smoked by Nikolai Kühn, not you. Besides, I imagine this pocket-watch is also his, as it doesn't quite match this dainty bedroom. And, judging by these fresh butts, I'd say he smoked them here not more than an hour ago. I'd like to know where he is."

"I can only repeat," she said with ill-concealed irritation, "that I have no idea where Kühn is, that I haven't seen him for a very long time, and that your suspicions are groundless. As for the chewed cigarette butts, I haven't read Conan Doyle for a long time and am not in a position to judge your deductive method. That's what it's called, if I'm not mistaken?"

She smiled caustically. We resumed our search. Kühn's suit was hanging in the wardrobe with a ticket of the Moscow-Leningrad express in one of the pockets. The notch on it indicated that he had come to Moscow two days before. I showed the ticket to Maria Fyodorovna and asked her if she thought this too had something to do with the deductive method.

"This suit and the railway ticket have nothing to do with Kühn. They belong to another man, a friend of mine. I'm not obliged to name him, since this concerns my private life. You may think whatever you like!"

We continued the search and found a man's raincoat, hat and shoes, which Maria Fyodorovna insisted belonged to her mysterious friend.

When we came to the kitchen I noticed that a large white kitchen buffet occupied a whole wall and asked Maria Fyodorovna what was behind it.

"Just the wall," she said and looked at the house porter, present as a witness during the search, rather strangely. The porter, an elderly, heavy-set man in a white apron, turned away, pretending he had not heard. I moved the buffet with assistants and found a door leading to a dark storage room. Maria Fyodorovna bit her lip nervously. I entered the room, piled high with old armchairs, broken chairs and chests. There was no one there apparently, but when I approached one of the cupboards I distinctly heard some one breathing.

"Won't you join us, Mister Kühn?!" I said, knocking on the door.

"One minute," the person inside answered in a deep voice; and then he came out: tall, stout, rosy-cheeked and bald with a small goatee, Kühn himself.

"There you are!" he said to Maria Fyodorovna. "You kept saying: 'Come to me and I'll kiss you, come to me and I'll kiss you.' Well, you certainly have. So you're the senior investigator who's been looking for me?" he asked in surprise, though still unruffled. "My, how young you are! I honestly envy you! Well, as the Russian saying goes: I've fallen into the pot like a chicken into the soup. But there's an Arabian saying that also fits the case: Listen to the advice of a woman and do the opposite. I should have done what the Arabs said! Now I've been punished. If only I had listened to wise Yanaki, who tried to talk me out of going to Leningrad. The old fox saw just what would happen. 'Nikolai,' he said, 'why go to the scene of the crime? So many have got into hot water that way!' "

"Then Yanaki's in Moscow?" I asked.

"He was two days ago. But I don't know where he is now. You'll never catch him, I'll bet anything on that!"

Kühn began to dress. Taking leave of Maria Fyodorovna, who clung to him bashfully, he said with a smile:

"Now, now, Mashet, *mein Liebling*, don't feel sad. You did kiss me after all, and it was worth risking everything for that alone. I'll get five years at most. After all, I was the one who offered the bribe, not the one who accepted it. *Auf Wiedersehn!*"

Kühn was a clever man who understood his position and kept his sense of humour. As soon as we were settled in my office he told me how he had bribed Ter-Avanesov and later brought Kraft into the deal.

"The untouchable Ter cost me thirteen thousand. Unfortunately, it didn't occur to me at the time that this was an unlucky number."

"Just a minute! Why thirteen thousand?" I asked.

"Ten thousand to Ter and three thousand to the middleman. I'm not sure what to call him."

"Do you mean his wife's lover?"

"Yes, Georgi-boy. I see you haven't been

wasting time while waiting for me. He wanted five thousand, but we finally agreed on three."

Kühn explained that he had just about lost all hope of ever finding "the key" to Ter-Avanesov, when suddenly he discovered that Ter-Avanesov's wife had a lover.

"*Cherchez la femme*, as the French say. I realized I now had a chance to find the key. A week later I became acquainted with this rake and discovered that I was not dealing with a Romeo or a Hamlet, but with a very ordinary scoundrel and pimp who would stoop to anything. We spent an evening together and figured out the whole scenario: the loss of a large sum of public funds, the possibility of suicide, and so on. I never doubted that Ter-Avanesov's wife would shake the last principles out of him when faced with such a situation. That very day I went to see Ter-Avanesov. And do you know, Citizen Inspector, I was almost sorry I had thought of such a plan when I saw how terrible he looked. But I had no other choice! Again, as the French say, *C'est la vie*—such is life!"

I took down his statement and was very glad that I now had the legal right to arrest the scoundrel who had played such a terrible role in Ter-Avanesov's life. That very evening "Georgi-boy"– Georgi Meilon–was arrested. True-to-type, he was a real coward. He shook as with a fever during the interrogation. He wept and lied, and lied and wept, and, in the end, confessed everything. It was established that the twenty-five thousand rubles he had received from his mistress in two instalments had been carefully put away in his bank account; to top his other fine points, he was phenomenally greedy and very stingy.

His sugary, servile face, insinuating voice, grovelling manner and protestations, his way of expressing himself in what he considered to be an elegant style, his shaved eyebrows and flashy suit aroused disgust and it was difficult to understand how Ter-Avanesov's wife could have succumbed to this professional pimp and tossed her love, her honour and the fate of her unhappy husband at his feet.

I was glad, too, that the scoundrel would get his due punishment; besides, his arrest would throw additional light on the roles played by Ter-Avanesov and Kühn.

It gave me great pleasure to send Meilon to jail. I had seen people whose crimes were far worse, but never before had I met a more despicable character. I had known murderers who had retained something human in spite of the terrible crimes they had committed. They were to pay the penalty for the crimes of which I, in line of duty, had proved them guilty; but they never aroused such burning contempt, such disgust as this greasy fop who sold himself and was capable of anything. I had seen robbers who undoubtedly would never have offered Meilon their hand had they known what I did. A jackal is not a tiger, needless to say, but how much more disgusting he is than a tiger!

Ter-Avanesov and the role he had played in the case were worthy of contempt; nevertheless, he was a victim of circumstances, one who had fallen into a trap set for him by Kühn and Meilon. The court took this into account and sentenced him to ten years imprisonment.

The Verbal Portrait

After Kühn had been apprehended, it remained to discover the whereabouts of the well-known Nepman Christopher Yanaki. Before disappearing from Leningrad, the scoundrel had had the foresight to destroy all his photographs, thus complicating the search no end.

According to Kühn, Yanaki was in Moscow, or, at any rate, had been there, and was using an alias he did not know.

My attempts to clear this question led to nothing. Meanwhile, we learned that Yanaki was one of the large grafters who had made a fortune in shady deals, and I was very pleased suddenly to receive word that he had been seen in one of the Leningrad suburbs on several occasions.

Pondering the ways of continuing the search, I decided to use the so-called "verbal portrait." This system was developed in 1885 by Alphonse Bertillon, a famous French anthropologist and director of the Institute of Identification of the Paris Police Prefecture. The system was later expanded by the Swiss criminologist Reiss, to whom, in 1912, the tsarist Ministry of Justice sent a group of Russian court investigators and criminologists to study.

A "verbal portrait," in the meaning accepted by criminologists, is an exact description of a person's appearance (his body, head and face) by means of special terminology. Obviously, a person describing the appearance of another does so by giving a verbal description of him. However, the common terms he uses cannot create a clear and accurate impression. Yet, in searching for a criminal, nothing less than an exact description of him will do.

According to the system of the verbal portrait, the profile is divided into three parts: the forehead, from the hairline to the bridge of the nose; the nose; and the mouth, from the base of the nose to the tip of the chin.

When conducting a search, or the identification of a criminal or a corpse by means of a verbal portrait, an investigator must use the exact terms intended for this purpose. With practice, a criminologist develops the ability to distinguish and remember the elements of the verbal portrait.

To establish Yanaki's verbal portrait, I had very carefully to question a large group of witnesses who gave me much useful information.

It then became clear that Yanaki was of medium height, heavy-set, with an oval face and low receding forehead, arched reddish eyebrows meeting over a long, hooked nose, a medium-size mouth drooping at the corners, thick lips, the lower of which was prominent, a square, cleft chin, large triangular, slightly protruding ears, puffy greenish eyes and red hair.

I had worked so hard over his verbal portrait that I imagined him quite clearly, though I had never seen him in my life. I sent this verbal portrait to the various departments, hoping that it would lead to the eventual capture of the elusive Yanaki. On Saturday I left for Sestroretsk, intending to spend the Sunday there. Sestroretsk was usually crowded on Sundays in those years, and on hot summer days the magnificent beach swarmed with bathers.

Next day, at the height of the bathing, I was lying on the beach beside two of my colleagues —inspectors Raginsky and Bodunov, when I noticed two young men strolling along, looking for someone.

"I think those boys are from the Transport Department," remarked Bodunov. "They seem to be looking for someone."

A few moments later they came up to us.

"Comrade Sheinin," said one of them, "we've come for you. The verbal portrait has done the job—we've got Yanaki in the militia station of the Detskoselsky Railway Station. The chief has asked you to come over. We went to your flat, but they said you were here."

Overjoyed, I threw on my clothes and was soon on my way to town. The militia chief was waiting for me at the Detskoselsky Station.

"You certainly gave us a hard time!" he said, evidently pleased with himself. "That's a cunning thing, a verbal portrait! I've never used it before. My boys have never heard of it either. Well, I called them all this morning, read them your verbal portrait, and we began to search for the red-headed guy."

"But where's Yanaki?" I asked impatiently.

"Well, there's at least a dozen there already," the chief answered happily and led me to the station room. "One of them is certainly Yanaki, and the others are probably his brothers."

A chill ran down my spine. The militia chief of the Detskoselsky Station was doing exactly the opposite of Bertillon and Reiss.

"Don't you understand," I cried, stammering from excitement, "that according to the verbal portrait, only *one* person can be arrested, and that this person can be no other than Yanaki."

"I won't argue," the jolly chief answered with a smile. "One of them definitely is Yanaki. I'm sure the others won't mind. We were very polite to them all. They're not in a cell, they're in the station room. Some are having tea, some are playing checkers and some are reading magazines. That's culture for you."

With a snort I rushed to the station room. It was aflame with dark-red, carrot-red and fiery-red-headed men, scurrying about, at a loss to understand what was happening. Their terror mounted with the appearance of every new red-head delivered by the boys of the Detskoselsky Station. The assistant chief, a young man in horn-rimmed glasses, was obviously excited by the possibilities of the verbal portrait. True, he met each new red-head politely enough, but immediately began carefully measuring and scrutinizing his ears, nose, the lines of his mouth and other elements of the verbal portrait, jotting mysterious notes in his little book and muttering something under his breath while the others looked on. To the red-headed men this was something like a mystical rite, especially since the assistant chief answered their questions very vaguely: "It all has to do with Bertillon and Reiss's verbal portrait. The Senior Inspector will soon be here and he'll decide everything. You'll have to wait till he comes."

None of the company had ever heard of Bertillon or Reiss, or the verbal portrait; and no one was having tea, playing checkers or reading magazines. The eldest, a butcher from Sennoy Market, who feared the revenue inspectors and taxes more than anything in the world, whispered to the others:

"It's all clear—they've fixed a special tax on red-heads, and we're done for!"

"What have taxes to do with it, stupid?" another protested. "They said quite clearly they're waiting for the inspector, and, mind you, a senior one. Besides, this fellow in the glasses is measuring everyone's nose and ears. Maybe you think there'll be different taxes for different noses?"

"You're both being childish," a third, formerly a stock-broker, rasped. "I'm sure they need red-headed men for some new film. And they're measuring our ears and noses to see if we fit the requirements."

I had come at the height of the argument apparently. The red-heads surrounded me and listened intently to my apologies. I explained, as I considered it my duty to do, that it was all a mistake, that we were looking for a fugitive who had red hair, but that the officers of the Detskoselsky Station had unfortunately been trying too hard. By checking their papers and applying the verbal portrait system, I soon saw that Yanaki was not among them. Once again I apologized and told them they were free. They scattered on the platform like a shower of autumn leaves. However, one of the red-heads remained behind. He signalled to me mysteriously and, taking me off to a side, whispered:

"While those three red-headed fools were busy guessing, I watched the assistant chief to see what noses and ears interested him most. I bet it's Yanaki's nose and ears he's looking for. He's not in Leningrad now. They say he's in Moscow. By the way, he loves to go to the operetta. That's all that I, speaking as a red-headed person, consider it my duty to offer in the way of assistance. Good afternoon, Comrade Senior Inspector."

He walked off with the air of a man who had done his civic duty.

Alone with the chief of the station, I told him what I thought of him and his "boys." He was very embarrassed and begged my pardon, saying: "From tomorrow I'll start studying criminology and really get the verbal portrait down pat." And indeed, a month later he came to me and rattled off the history of the verbal portrait, its terminology, the scheme and method of its development. He quoted Bertillon and Reiss, Weingardt and Yakimov, and concluded:

"I need only close my eyes to visualize that damn Yanaki who put me in such an awkward position. To say nothing of the reprimand I got from my chief for all those red-heads. But Bertillon was a clever fellow! That verbal portrait he thought up is really worth something!"

The day after the chief of the Detskoselsky Station had demonstrated his achievements in criminology, a letter addressed to me was received at the Regional Court. It was from Yanaki himself and read as follows:

"Dear Senior Inspector Sheinin,

"You seem to be dying to see me. I can't say I share your feelings, and true love is bliss only when it is mutual. It gave me a good laugh to hear how you were looking for me according to some foolish verbal portrait thought up by one Professor Reiss. A lot I care about that professor and his verbal portrait!

"*Adieu!*
"*Yanaki.*"

Now I was really angry. This Nepman swindler was not only evading the law, but ridiculing the science of criminology! I showed the Regional Procurator this original document and, drawing his attention to the fact that the letter had been post-marked "Moscow," asked for permission to go there at once. I had no clear notion of what I would do to find Yanaki, but I was counting on the help of my old friends in MUR. The Regional Procurator was just as nettled by the letter as I and told me to start immediately.

The very next day I was in MUR, in Osipov's office, telling him and the others what had happened to Yanaki's verbal portrait. Then I showed them the letter. Osipov reddened with anger.

"Boys," he said to his assistants, "are we going to let a lousy Nepman, a grafter and speculator, laugh at criminology and justice? What do you think we should do?"

"Can there be any doubt about it?" Tylner, always calm, correct and self-assured, asked. "First of all, we have his verbal portrait. Then we know that Yanaki frequents the operetta like most Nepmen, which means we have to look in at the Aquarium and the Hermitage. Finally, he's a furniture man, and must certainly have some friends among the Moscow furniture dealers. We should look into this, too. And as the whole thing has become a matter of principle, our group ought to take part in the general search for Yanaki.

"Right you are," Nozhnitsky said in his usual soft voice. "We'll have to spend our evenings at the operetta, taking turns seeing *The Queen of Czardas* and *Die Fledermaus*. There's no other way."

"That's that," Osipov concluded and rose to show that the conference was over. "What's at the Aquarium today?"

Nozhnitsky picked up his paper, looked through the ads and said it was *The Queen of Czardas*, with Tatyana Bach, Bravin and Yaron in the main roles.

Osipov and I went to the Aquarium Summer Garden that evening to see a performance of *The Queen of Czardas*. Our seats were in the third row, on the right. Several rows behind us sat two of Osipov's assistants: Yasha Saksagansky, a thin young Georgian with a small black moustache, who was considered an expert on verbal portraits, and Vanya Bezrukov, always laughing and gay, with mischievous grey eyes that could look both frontwards and backwards, as they said in MUR.

When Osipov and I were strolling by the puny lindens of the Aquarium during the first intermission, Saksagansky came up to us and said:

"Here's how things are: there are twelve red-heads watching the performance. Two pairs of ears are right, but their noses are wrong. Three have the noses we want, but the ears are wrong. We've no luck at all with the hanging lips; only one red-head's lip protrudes a little, and that's nothing because he was smoking a pipe; anyone's lip is liable to stick out when smoking a pipe."

This piece of news reminded me of the waiting-room at the Detskoselsky Station. However, my worries were unfounded. I was dealing with Osipov this time, and felt the difference immediately.

"Yasha," Osipov interrupted, "your report reminds me of the bride in Gogol's play *The Marriage*. The scatter-brain in that play also dreamed of combining the nose of one suitor with the lips of another. I'm not interested in your stock of the noses, Comrade Saksagansky. I only want one nose, the one that belongs to Christopher Yanaki. Now tell me: is that nose here today, or not?"

"I'll have the answer to that by the second intermission," Yasha promised.

"Check the second row on the left," Osipov said. "We're too far away, but I thought there was someone there who.... Anyway, have a look at the second row, Yasha."

During the second act, needless to say, I was looking less at the stage than at the second row on the left, where someone's fiery-red head blazed between a bald one as shiny as a billiard ball and a woman's fluffy, intricate coiffure. As it was some distance away, I could not have a good look at the ears, nose and mouth, but saw Yasha walk by twice with his hand on his cheek, like a man with a toothache.

During the second act, when Edwin and Silva, arms around each other, began the famous duet which brought up the vital question: "Do you recall how happiness smiled on us?", it actually did smile on me, because Yasha appeared in the aisle at that moment, and breathed hot into my ear:

"I think Yanaki's sitting in the sixth row. There's one inconsistency, but everything else matches. I'll resign tomorrow if it isn't Yanaki. I'll point him out during the intermission."

I immediately passed the information to Osipov. Not a muscle of his face moved. Nodding his head in time to the music like a true lover of the arts, he answered softly:

"I'm afraid Yasha's jumping to conclusions. Still, anything is possible. We'll see during the intermission."

The second act over, Osipov took my arm and we strolled through the brightly lit paths, mixing with the well-dressed, animated crowd. This was a typical Moscow Aquarium crowd of the time. Smartly dressed women floated past in summer wraps trimmed with silver fox and sable. Their eyes were heavily made-up and their painted lips burned unnaturally against their thickly powdered cheeks. Red-faced grocers and fish merchants from Zatsepa solemnly escorted their high-bosomed round-faced wives in printed silk Persian shawls with long fringes swishing the ground. Portly middle-aged manufacturers from Nikolskaya and Petrovka streets displayed their stylish pince-nez and gold teeth. Young dandies in short, narrow trousers and tight-fitting plaid blazers, then the height of fashion, trailed in droves after the affected young ladies with boyish bobs and daring bangs on their tiny foreheads.

Suddenly I noticed a man with hair of a striking black strolling beside a luscious blonde in a white cape, a blue-fox thrown casually over her arm. His face seemed familiar, though I was positive I had never seen him.

I peered at his companion's dyed hair, which had the dull peroxide look, and suddenly realized what made the man's face seem so familiar: he had a fleshy hooked nose, a low, receding forehead, bushy knitted eyebrows, a square, cleft chin and red triangular ears —everything that fitted Yanaki's verbal portrait!

Seeing him smoke, I quickly approached and asked for a light. He slowly drew a box of matches from his pocket and lit one. I looked at his hands and my heart began to thump— they were freckled and covered with thick red fuzz. A look at his face showed that his puffy eyes were light-green and his eyelashes red. Yes, this was Yanaki, but he had dyed his hair.

Drawing back, I saw Yasha standing close by with a vacant expression and the absent-minded look of one who cared nothing for Yanaki, the Aquarium Summer Garden, the operetta *The Queen of Czardas* or even whether he was going to resign tomorrow morning or not.

Coming closer, he whispered:

"I'm glad you've also noticed that dyed gobbler. If that's not Yanaki, I'm an ass!"

Dear, poor Yasha! Several years later he died of tuberculosis. When they carried the coffin out of his small bachelor's room (he had never married, for he knew he was ill), his colleagues followed deeply grieved. They had really loved this brave, kind and hot-tempered man, devoted to their difficult profession to the end.

I had another look at the "black edition" of Yanaki and whispered to Osipov that I thought Yasha was right; the man's hair had a strange purple tint.

"Quite possible," Osipov said with affected indifference, but grasping my arm tighter. "It's quite likely that the scoundrel has dyed his hair. That's probably what makes him so cheeky. But we have to be doubly sure, I don't care to share the laurels of the Detskoselsky Station chief. If he does turn out to be Yanaki and we've snared him the very first evening, I'll begin to believe in the Hereafter and in the fact that old Bertillon and Reiss have been plotting in Heaven to help us catch him in punishment for ridiculing their system."

Osipov and I were not in our seats when the curtain went up again. We stood by the wall near the sixth row, watching the black-haired suspect. Osipov had gone backstage a few minutes before, and returned looking very pleased. Mysteriously, he whispered that we were about to see a "curious psychological experiment."

My sharp-witted friend had decided to make doubly sure of his suspect with the aid of the operetta *The Queen of Czardas* itself—strange as it may seem. Knowing that operetta actors were great improvisors, often adding lines of their own, Osipov had persuaded them to add a few words to the scene in which Edwin's father was shocked to learn that Madame Volapük had been a variety-stage singer in her youth, featured as "The Nightingale." Osipov asked her to add only that she was also the daughter of the furniture dealer Yanaki.

The audience, naturally, paid no attention to this minor detail, but the jet-black head in the sixth row jerked nervously and its owner, deciding that he had probably heard wrong, bent to his companion to ask what name had been spoken.

"It's him!" Osipov said with a sigh of relief. "Yasha's worth his weight in gold. And good for you for having developed Yanaki's verbal portrait so well! Come on, we'll greet him at the exit."

An hour later a very confused Yanaki was sitting in Osipov's office, unable to grasp that he had actually been caught by a verbal portrait though he had dyed his hair.

"Well, Yanaki," Osipov said, "I hope you've realized that Professor Reiss was cleverer than you and that law-breakers should never laugh at such a science as criminology."

"I've realized it all right, but too late, Inspector," he answered glumly. "My letter was much too nervy, and I'd like you to note that in your report. When I was a boy my father used to say: 'Christopher, you don't respect science enough and nothing good will ever come of that.' Tell me, Inspector, how could a man as wise as my father have had such a stupid son, and how could such an idiot as I have had such a father? What's happened to the laws of heredity? How do you think the science of criminology and Professor Reiss, whom I now respect so much, would explain all this?"

"I'm quite willing to discuss these very reasonable questions," Osipov answered, "but only after you've served your sentence. And now, to borrow an expression of yours— *adieu*!"

And that is how Bertillon and Reiss' verbal portrait was fully vindicated.

1956

ACKNOWLEDGEMENT OF GUILT*

There have been more and more news items about people who voluntarily came to militia stations to plead guilty to various crimes.

People of different ages, professions and backgrounds—out-and-out robbers with years of experience, nimble pick-pockets, embezzlers and murderers—they tell of crimes that have gone undetected.

Not all of them, of course, reached the decision to acknowledge their guilt easily and quickly. But reach it they did nevertheless.

A jeweller with a peg-leg came to a militia station, saying that he had worked in the gold and jewel department of a large store for a

* This story was published in the March 16, 1937, issue of *Izvestia*. The events which resulted from its publication are described in the two following stories: *Making a Clean Breast of It* and *A Firm Handshake*.

long time, that he had managed all sorts of shrewd combinations, tampering with the books and stealing over a period of years. Much time had passed. The store had long since been closed down. He had never been apprehended or even suspected. And yet one evening, there he was at the militia station. Haltingly and in great confusion he confessed to everything. He unscrewed his hollow leg and from a hidden compartment dumped a pile of stolen diamonds and gold on to the officer's desk.

What had caused his sudden confession?

"Don't you understand? I got this peg-leg fighting for the Soviet Republic and I'm ashamed to use it for hiding the jewels I stole from the Soviet Republic. And then, it's not too easy to sell them."

If this had happened in another country, the reporters would certainly have pursued the man; there would certainly have been interviews with all his relatives and friends, and he would have been the hero of the day. In our country, however, no one was especially surprised at the event.

In 1937 the Procurator of the U.S.S.R. received the following letter from Byelorussia. One Yasenko, a village school teacher, wrote:

"...I'm very well settled here and no one would ever dream of suspecting me of anything. On the contrary, I am sincerely liked and respected. But believe me, that only makes things worse. For the past year I have been leading an honest, hard-working and ordered existence. I have been here a year and could stay indefinitely. I have never felt happier than now, and that is exactly why I am writing to you, Comrade Procurator. My name is not Yasenko at all, and I settled here after escaping from prison. Long ago I graduated from a pedagogical school, and this helped me find work in a profession I had almost forgotten. I had to use forged documents, of course. But I have come to love my work and would like to dedicate my life to teaching, after I've served the rest of my sentence. Please tell me where and how to come...."

Several days later, the writer of these lines was in the office of the Procurator of the U.S.S.R. He spoke of himself shyly and simply. He had a pleasant young face and a sad smile.

"I find it difficult to analyze my feelings," he said. "However, one thing is quite clear: there can be no return to the past. I was a bandit, a robber and a criminal, but I've tried to live honestly for a year and now I find I can't live otherwise. But I must be consistent. I have a small debt to pay. I was sentenced to five years for robbery, and escaped after serving several months. I've decided to pay my debt first and enter my new life with clean hands."

Then he gave a detailed account of all the robberies and burglaries he had taken part in, naming dates, cities and places.

He had never liked to stay in one town long and covered a great area in several years.

"When I came to Byelorussia and found work as a teacher, I thought it would be awfully dull, since I was used to changing cities and climates and seeing new faces all the time. I liked excitement, but now I had the school, the children, the snow-covered fields, the silence and very few people. And do you know, it was quite different from what I had expected. Never before had I been so content. It may sound strange, but it's the truth. It was most awkward to teach geography," Yasenko said and smiled. "I'd start talking about the

Black Sea coast and recall the burglaries I had committed there. Telling the children about Siberia, I'd remember a robbery in Omsk."

He was sent to a labour colony to finish his sentence and is working there now in his new and last profession of a teacher.

The "autobiography" of Ivan Frolov began without introduction or ado, in a business-like, even concise manner:

> *To the Procurator of the U.S.S.R.*
> *from Ivan Frolov, a recidivist*

AUTOBIOGRAPHY

"I, Ivan Frolov, born in the city of Saratov in 1911, hereby inform you, the Procurator of the U.S.S.R., that I have no papers whatever at present. Fearing this might land me in jail, I have decided to appeal to the highest authority, the Procurator of the U.S.S.R. I am certain that you would give special attention to this statement from a recidivist thief if you were to hear of it or read it yourself. I think that you will take the necessary steps to help—I don't want to say *me*, but a thief with a new outlook developed by the new Constitution, one who has read your speech at the congress and come to the conclusion that, to put it briefly, all tramps have come to the end of their ropes.

"The following is an outline of my life and of the reasons which made me start on the wrong road. When you have read these lines, you will see what made me come to my senses and decide to live honestly.

"As I said before, I was born in the city of Saratov and was brought up by a stranger. I lived with my step-mother, a housewife. My father, a Volga stevedore, died of hunger in 1921...."

Frolov went on to tell of his early years as a waif, how he learned to steal, and became adept in his profession.

"...I followed life's crooked road. I lived in the street, my friends were thieves, and I led a drunken life. I frequented the Sukharevsky Market, expensive restaurants and cafés, the cinema, and other places where money was needed. That is how I spent a year and a half in Moscow, until arrested by MUR and later sentenced. I have decided to appeal to you personally. I am leading a parasitic existence among strangers now and ask you, the Supreme Procurator, to give me your help, to give me a new pass to life.

"Please send me to any town or village to work and lead an honest life, to be a useful Soviet citizen. I despise the life I've been leading, because I have realized that one can live well by working honestly and being a useful member of society.

"Signing my name to this, I assure you of my sincerity,

"*Ivan Frolov.*"

Out of cunning or shyness Frolov added the following postscript instead of his address:

"I would be grateful if you published the answer to this letter in *Izvestia*, stating your opinion and just what is done in such cases. The point is: do I have to go to jail and labour camp first or can I do without them?"

The Procurator of the U.S.S.R. has authorized me to answer your letter, Ivan Frolov.

You may come to the Procurator's Office any day in the week. Your matter will be discussed and all possible help given.

I am sure that Ivan Frolov will come to the office. He will come because a new way of life and new human relationship are unfolding around him. His incentive to come, therefore, will be stronger than the fear of punishment, stronger than his old habits, than anything in the world.

1937

MAKING A CLEAN BREAST OF IT

It all began on March 16th.

At exactly 10 a.m. the commandant on duty at the office of the Procurator of the U.S.S.R. was approached by a sharp-eyed youth. Holding out a copy of *Izvestia* he inquired quite simply:

"Where are the thieves supposed to report?"

The commandant looked at him in surprise.

"I don't understand you, citizen. What actually did you have in mind?"

"It's a personal matter. I've come about the notice in the paper. To confess."

He was finally directed to a certain room and set out for the fourth floor. There he carefully read the names on the doors, looked up and down, and sat down on a couch in the waiting-room. The secretary asked him whom he wished to see.

"I've come to see Sheinin," the youth answered calmly. "But I'd rather not go in yet. I'll wait a bit. Some more fellows ought to be along soon."

"Are you all going in together?"

"No, it's just that we'd feel more easy if we were all together. It's more certain and less worrisome that way, you know."

And he made himself comfortable. Half an hour later a man in a brown jacket with a collar of cat's fur entered. He looked round, sat down beside the youth, lit a cigarette, took a long drag, and said indifferently, addressing no one in particular:

"I think I recognize your face. We were in a camp in Siberia together if I'm not mistaken."

"You're wrong," said the youth smiling, and then added. "We were in another camp together. Unfortunately, I was in the Siberian camp after you'd left."

That's how their conversation began. While they were recalling "the good old days," all sorts of deals and prisons, three others entered the room.

Though they were strangers, the conversation picked up quickly and effortlessly as they discussed the problem uppermost in their minds.

"You can bet your life they'll jail us," said a stoop-shouldered, glum-looking man in his forties. "I know their tricks. They think they can catch us like one-year-old donkeys. Listen to me, boys, and don't go in. If Turman says so, he knows what he's talking about."

"What did you come here for, if you're so smart?"

A sly smile crossed Turman's face and he said:

"The boys sent me over to get the low-down on this deal. What a joke—they write about it in the papers and send us an invite. Like hell that Frolov wrote them and they were answering him. Which Frolov? Why Frolov? And who the hell knows him? It's all a fake, you can take my word for it! But I'd like to know why they cooked the whole thing up. I, for one, have never heard of Frolov. If there is such a fellow, why don't they give his nickname?"

Meanwhile, more and more people were coming in. Recognizing "their own kind" unerringly and at a glance, they joined them.

When there were eleven men in the waiting-room, a tall, well-dressed, clean-shaven man with excellent manners got the assembly in hand. It was obvious that he knew his own worth and was used to giving orders. He was immediately accepted as the boss. His name was Kostya the Count.

"Stop blabbing, let's get down to business," he said. "We're not babies and there's no use wasting time on philosophy. I don't know what this is all about. I see that everyone here has a copy of *Izvestia*, and they are all yesterday's papers for some reason. That's a strange coincidence! The situation's clear. I don't give a damn whether there is a Frolov or not. Supposing there's not. But there are Turman, Cockroach, the King, Gypsy, me, and the rest of you, aren't there? Yes, there are. Then what's wrong? If Turman doesn't believe in this thing, he can pack up and leave. But I do believe in it. And I'm going in. Am I risking a lot? Yes, I am. But what actually are we risking, my dears? They can do what they want to us. It's about time to wind things up anyway. It doesn't really matter if they throw us in the jug; and if they don't we're that much better off. In any case, I'm tying the knot. I'm out of the game. I've come to the finish. I've had enough. Am I right or wrong?"

"You're right, Count," they answered together.

And even the glum Turman added:

149

"I'm in with the rest. If you all go in, I'll go in, too."

An hour later we were all friends. The eleven of them sat in my office, each telling of his life in turn.

"I'm a burglar and have been in the business eight years," said Cockroach. "I've already had a couple of convictions and many arrests. I've seen and tried everything: cocaine in Moscow, *tiriak* and *anash* in Bukhara, and opium in Vladivostok. I've been in jail and out again, I starved and threw money around like a playboy. But this past year I've become restless. Everywhere people are like people: they work, they live, they have professions, they get married and have children. Why am I worse than they? I want to live like everyone else. No sense in lying, I've stolen during this past year, too. Just two days ago I stole a leather coat from the University. But that's all. Believe me. I'm not pulling your leg. If it's at all possible, I wish you wouldn't book me. Give me a town, some papers and a job. You'll see, I'll go straight."

Cockroach fell to thinking and then added suddenly, blushing:

"I want to be happy. Believe me that thieves

never live happy lives. I was only happy once, and even then it was in my dreams."

"What did you dream about?"

Cockroach smiled wistfully and said:

"I once dreamt that I was a very young, but expert thief. It was spring, a lovely day, the sun was shining, there were flowers and all such stuff. I was walking along, straight from a job, carrying a big bundle. It was bright daylight and I was walking down Stoleshnikov Street. There were big crowds, and all the girls were smiling. A militiaman stood on the corner of Stoleshnikov and Petrovka streets, an ordinary militiaman in white gloves. Opposite him was a huge store with a fancy sign: 'Moscow Department Store, Stolen Articles Bought.' Can you imagine such a wonderful thing? And I walked past the militiaman with my bundle, and it was all legal. The director of the store himself met me at the door. He took all the junk cordially and according to the price list, and said most politely: 'We haven't seen you in a long time. I'll never fulfil my plan this way.'"

Gypsy was a young, cleanly dressed girl with mischievous eyes. She said she had been born in Odessa, a thief since she was fourteen.

She had a daughter in Odessa whom her sister was bringing up. Her husband was also a thief, but she had come to my office alone.

"My husband's waiting for the results in Serpukhov," she said. "He's afraid this is a trap. He sent me over to see if there's anything phony about the deal. He says that if anything goes wrong, they'll be lenient because I'm a woman and will give me less time, while he'll be able to earn a bit for parcels for me. He says if it's all above board, I should send him a wire at once and he'll come too."

The Spinning Top, a nimble, laughing pickpocket whose nickname fitted him well, handed me a sheet of paper.

"Here, I've put it all down. You read it. I'll add something to it later."

This is what he had written:

Days of Crime.

"I finished seven-year school in 1931 when I was still a young man of fifteen. I had no profession. When my father died in 1932 I felt I was on my own. I met some 'nice' boys who dragged me down into their rotten company and taught me their criminal ways, i.e., thieving, playing cards and drinking. Three years after I began my life as a thief, I got caught and was sentenced. I finished my term in September 1936 and decided to change my ways and become a useful citizen. But no matter how I tried to become a useful citizen, I just couldn't make it. I swear I'll succeed this time and shall breathe the same air as all the other citizens of our socialist land. I don't want to be a weed in the fertile field of our country.

"Top."

"Please don't print my name, because I have a girl-friend and I don't want her to know about this. She can find out later, when all this has become part of my past."

Kostya the Count spoke with dignity, slowly and without sentimentality. His manner was sober and business-like.

"I'm getting on in years," he said. "I'm thirty-eight now and have seen more in my lifetime than these greenhorns ever dreamt of. Mine is a real and highly skilled speciality. There are hardly any of us left now. My beat was the Moscow-Manchuria express. My partner's a rare beauty! Her name's Wanda and she's quite the lady in her seal-skin coat. As for me, I always wear horn-rimmed glasses in the train to look more impressive. Yes, I was always very presentable. Naturally, we only rode first-class, and always pretended to be strangers. Then some rich fop or other would strike up a friendship with Wanda. You know what those travelling acquaintanceships are. Wanda never refused their attentions. Then they would have tea together or drink wine in the dining car at supper. She'd slip a sleeping powder into his drink and when he'd fall asleep, we'd pick up his luggage and get off at the first stop. Understand? But the past two years have been very hard and I've hardly been able to do anything in my line. The travellers' cheques have spoilt it all, because no one carries cash any more. It's hard to change a profession at my age (though I am not really *that* old); there's no sense in it, and I don't care to. And, to tell you the truth, I'm fed up with the whole business. I've done a few odd jobs here and there in the interim, no use being modest or playing the fool. But I'm here now to tell you about it, and I am not stupid enough to think I'll get a prize for it. I have a side-line by the way. I'm a first-rate surveyor. I wish you'd send me off with some expedition, as far away as possible. I'm afraid to stay in Moscow just now; the temptation to fall back into my old way of life might be too great. If you help me, I'll go off with an expedition, stay away a couple of years, go straight, and come back to Moscow, only when I'm sure of myself. That's about all."

The others spoke in much the same vein. When they had all been questioned, they were received by Comrade Vyshinsky.

They asked for various jobs in different cities and were promised such work.

There was a strange meeting at the *Izvestia* editorial offices that evening. Besides the recidivists who had been at the Procurator's Office that morning, there were many more. Their number had grown like a snowball rolling downhill, and the group that arrived was many times larger than in the morning.

Unfortunately, there was a small misunderstanding. At first, it had been agreed that they would come at 7 p.m., but then the editors could not see them until 11 p.m. Many were frightened by this, suspecting a trap.

Kostya the Count phoned me to tell what was happening.

"Let's have it straight," he said. "Are you or are you not going to run us in? Many of the boys, and I too, will come just the same, but some of the chaps are growing doubtful. Can I give them my word that they're in no danger?"

I assured him that he could, and they all came. Once in the office, they grew calmer, and seeing that no one wanted to "run them in," became talkative.

A man they called "King" said he had come as a delegate from a small but tightly knit gang of pick-pockets who had talked it over and sent him to the editorial offices to see what would come of the whole affair.

"The boys are keeping a sharp eye on the goings on, and they'll probably all come to-morrow. And anyway, there's no other way out. We want to live like everybody else, and the militia won't give us a moment's peace. The inspectors are getting far too sharp for us!"

Then the meeting began; it was a unique conference conducted by the Procurator of the U.S.S.R. and the editors of the newspaper.

The talk was plain and to the point. The Procurator said that law was law and that making a clean breast of it did not imply they would get off scott-free.

"You've come here of your own free will,"

he said. "We won't arrest anyone who has come here to make a clean breast of it. We'll help you find jobs and give you an opportunity to start life anew. It won't come easy, don't count on that. There may be many difficulties and much wavering. But we hope that you will keep your word. The future depends on yourselves, and I think it will be a happy future."

Kostya the Count spoke on behalf of the recidivists, and was visibly moved as he said:

"It may be strange to hear this from me, but if a thief gives you his word of honour, it's really his word of honour. It's metal, stainless steel, it's platinum! We all vouch for each other. You may be sure that it will be exactly as we say."

Cockroach and Turman were busily writing something in a far corner, arguing in subdued voices about the wording. Finally, they had finished. It was a strange appeal to all professional thieves on behalf of those recidivists present and read as follows:

"Comrades Criminals, you who are still living in the streets! Look around and see what the Soviet Government has been doing for us. Can't we really understand

157

what's expected of us? It's high time we realized that the Soviet Union is offering its proletarian hand to drag us out of the sewer. Away with your doubts and suspicions! Follow our example! Get jobs and stop thieving. Nothing good will come of stealing anyway. Don't disgrace your country. Be worthy sons of our Motherland!"

1937

A FIRM HANDSHAKE

They were leaving Moscow from various railway stations on a mild evening in March. These were the first of the lot, the first thirteen who had come to the Procurator's Office. Actually, only twelve were leaving. The thirteenth, Kostya the Count, was staying in Moscow for a time, but would soon start for the Arctic.

Each of the travellers had a treasured document in his breast pocket: a letter of recommendation to his new town and new job, where a new life waited for him with difficult tests.

Kostya the Count hurried from station to station, buying the tickets, seeing his friends to their seats, and grimly admonishing them. Never had his existence been so busy, difficult, happy and full.

"Make sure you don't turn out to be rats, boys," he warned. "Don't let the others down, and don't let yourselves down! They'll judge everyone by us. We can spoil a big thing, but it's up to us to make it go. Make something of it, for Christ's sake! Croak, but don't go wrong. Cry your eyes out, but don't steal. Better chop your hands off, than lose control of them. I think you understand."

Yes, they understood him. They had become very fond of him; they trusted him, and his word was law.

As they stood in a queue for tickets at the Kiev Railway Station, Cockroach's eyes fell unwittingly on the near-sighted woman standing beside him. She was squinting helplessly, seeking someone in the crowd. Her two elegant suitcases stood dully shining by a column. The look of them wrung Cockroach's heart! They seemed to be waiting to be picked up. Cockroach reddened with the struggle within him, trying to turn his eyes from those accursed suitcases. Kostya the Count caught his fixed gaze.

"What's the matter, Cockroach?" he whispered ferociously. "Do you want to sink with those lousy bags and drag twelve others with you?"

Cockroach turned purple and began to swear it wasn't so.

"Why, no, Kostya," he said. "You hurt me, saying such things. But look at those suitcases and look at the way that foolish woman is standing there. They're just an eyesore, that's what they are."

"An eyesore!" Kostya snapped. "May your eyes burst altogether, if such kind of junk makes them sore. Put sand on them or salt!"

And then, approaching the absent-minded lady, he bowed with a flourish and said in a sugary voice: "Pardon me, Madam, you seem to be waiting for someone? I think it my duty to warn you to keep an eye on your bags before someone walks off with them. There are all kinds of muggers about in the railway stations ... ah, excuse me, I meant thieves, and you'd better keep a close eye on your belongings."

The lady gasped, clutched her suitcases and dashed off.

"An ounce of prevention, boys," Kostya said with a smile. "It's a great thing, when you think of it."

Meanwhile, the number of people arriving at the Procurator's Office was rapidly mounting. A special commission was set up at MUR.

Each newcomer was checked and interviewed before the commission decided where he was to be sent.

When several escaped convicts turned up, they were told quite frankly:

"Those of you who have not served your full terms will have to do so. A confession does not relieve you of punishment. Go to MUR, tell them you escaped from prison and they'll send you back. Give yourselves up. We trust you."

Every one of them showed up at MUR that day and was sent back to finish his sentence.

There were several embezzlers among our callers. One, named Salikov, appeared at the Procurator's Office in the evening quite the worse for drink. The superintendent showed him into my office.

"I've come to make a clean breast of it," he said in an unsteady voice. "My name is Salikov. I'd like to tell you that I owe seventeen thousand. I'm living under a false name. It's sad, but true!"

He was told that one should come in sober to make one's confession and was let out with the suggestion that he go home, have a good night's sleep and return in the morning.

The commandant was sorry to let him go.

He was afraid that Salikov would never return when sober.

But come back he did. He appeared in the morning and began with a confused apology for his appearance the previous evening.

"Please excuse me," he said. "To tell you the truth, I had to have a few drinks to get up courage. You know, it's a bit strange to pack your own self off to jail."

Then he told us his simple story. He had worked in various offices and had embezzled seventeen thousand rubles. A fugitive from justice, he had lived on forged papers until he decided to confess his crime.

Told that he was to be arrested and tried, he accepted the news calmly.

"I never counted on anything else. I'll be sentenced and serve my time, and then be free. I don't consider myself a lost soul."

Dozens of others repeated his words, saying they did not consider themselves lost to the world. This perhaps was the real meaning behind the unique movement that had begun among these people. They were all guided by the conviction that there could be no lost souls, no stepchildren in our country and society.

The phone rang and someone said in a choked voice:

"I wonder if you could see me. I'm neither a thief nor a bandit, but worse! My name is Rybin."

A few minutes later he walked into my office. He was tall, had a mass of blond hair and curiously fixed eyes. His face seemed much older than that of a man of twenty-four. He avoided my eyes as he spoke, and seemed to be listening to his own voice; his sentences were confused, his words came out with difficulty.

"I killed two people," he said. "That was long ago. But not so very long ago either. The first in Skopino in 1930. I shot him in the back. It was near the railway tracks. He was a rat. A terrible person. Am I making myself clear?"

Leading questions brought the distorted picture into focus. He apparently realized that he was being incoherent and often stopped to ask: "Am I making myself clear?"

He had committed the second crime in 1932 in Central Asia. Then a meteorologist at a mountain observatory, he had quarrelled with one of the workers at the station and pushed him over a cliff.

After Rybin had told his story to me, the Procurator saw him, listened to it again and said:

164

"All right, Rybin. We'll check everything, and investigate the facts. You've done the right thing by coming to us with your burden."

Rybin smiled for the first time and answered:

"That's what it is, a great burden. It's been pressing on me terribly. I'm worn out. And when I read in the papers that even professional criminals were coming in to confess, I said to myself: how can I stay away?"

He was arrested, and the case was handed over to an investigator to determine the motives and circumstances of his crimes.

Avesyan phoned from the reception room and said, enunciating each syllable.

"I'd like you to see me. I need assistance of a special kind. Mine is a very unusual case."

Presently he came in, a well-built and dark-eyed man, and when he spoke it was in a calm manner, slightly rolling his "r's."

"Just imagine," he said. "I'm mad about psychiatry. Besides, I want you to note that I like the theatre. I believe that a true actor must be a good psychiatrist. My one desire is to become an actor and I will some day. I can just see myself as Othello. Believe me, I'll be much better than Papasyan."

When I interrupted to ask what his artistic inclinations had to do with the Procurator's Office, Avesyan flushed and said:

"Pardon me, I seem to have strayed from the point. I'm a swindler by profession. But in my heart, I repeat, I'm a tragic actor. I've never been caught. Several times I pretended I was mentally unbalanced, but just for fun. I always studied the symptoms of the illness in question beforehand, and never made a false step. The doctors always diagnosed my case according to the symptoms. You realize, of course, that this was done solely for the sake of practice, just to practise acting. Here, I'll recite for you." He proceeded to recite a monologue from Othello with great feeling. Then we spoke of psychiatry, of Descartes, Mach, Bekhterev, Freud and others, and I found that he was probably as well informed in this field as many a young psychiatrist.

He was sent to the Committee on Arts and interviewed. Finding that he was really gifted, they enrolled him in the Lunacharsky Theatre Institute.

The days passed and there was no end to the stream of people passing through the reception room of the Procurator's Office and then on to MUR, where they were always met with sympathy.

Criminals from other cities followed the example of Moscow. In Leningrad, Kiev, Sverdlovsk, Kharkov, Yaroslavl and other cities they came to the Procurator's Offices and the militia stations to confess their crimes and state their readiness to sever all ties with their criminal past.

On March 26, a certain M. came to the Procurator's Office of the Ukrainian S.S.R. in Kiev and, producing the March 18th and 20th issues of *Izvestia*, said:

"I've come in connection with this."

He sighed and told the long story of his past. He had been a professional thief, a house breaker, fence and swindler for twenty-five years.

He had been in Austria, Belgium and Yugoslavia before the Revolution, had carried off most of his robberies successfully and had only been sentenced twice in his entire career.

Using forged documents a short time ago, M. had got a job in Kiev. Though quite content with his work, he had decided to come to the Procurator's Office and confess.

"I've been thinking about those articles I've read day and night. They've upset me badly and I've decided to come and tell you everything. You can do as you please," he said.

Similar statements were being made in Procurator's Offices throughout the country.

The following telegram, addressed to the Procurator of the U.S.S.R., was received from Kungur:

> "Awaiting permission to come as a delegate from the Kungur recidivists. Wire reply. Khrapov. 21 Sverdlov Street, Kungur."

A wire was sent to Khrapov to the effect that he need not come to Moscow. He could appear at the local Procurator's Office and would find the necessary advice and aid.

Most of those who came to confess their crimes were sent to work in various towns. MUR began sending the former recidivists to work. The All-Union Council of Trade Unions took an active part in getting jobs for those who wished to sever all ties with their criminal past.

The first duty of the trade unions, Komsomol and other civic organizations was to receive these people in the right spirit. They had to be helped to settle in their new towns, to be given proper attention and drawn into public affairs. Instead of petty-bourgeois commiseration and common curiosity, they were offered a hand of help and friendship, a welcoming hand to all who had triumphed in the most difficult and tortuous struggle—the struggle with themselves.

1937

THE HUNTING KNIFE

The papers were finally signed and there it stood, black on white, that A. Burov, Professor of Zoology, and his assistant Voronov were being sent to Kolguyev Island in the Barents Sea to conduct scientific research for a period of one year.

Their colleagues at the university read the notice and laughed. The teachers and students knew only too well that the professor and his assistant could not bear the sight of each other. The news that these two were to be sent to a deserted island for a year, where they would be thrown together twenty-four hours a day, prompted a shrug and a smile. Some said it had been done on purpose, a scheme to cool their tempers with the harsh climate.

"They'll come back friends," they said. "Just you wait and see, they'll be the best of pals."

But the two most surprised by the news were the men involved. It became known at the university, that the professor had spent a sleepless night when he discovered the name of his companion for the winter. And Voronov was no less upset.

Still, orders were orders, and several days later the university team consisting of Professor Burov and Assistant Professor Voronov set out for an island in the far-off Barents Sea, where they were to spend a long Arctic year together.

Their first letters arrived a month later. They wrote of their first impressions, the details of their journey, and their plans for the future.

"Everything would be fine," read the professor's letter, "if not for the constant presence of this character, who can definitely be qualified as a subject for scientific study by any zoologist. This young man continues to get on my nerves. Being here and unfortunately having to see him constantly, I am once again convinced that my original dislike of him was well founded."

Voronov, in turn, complained of "the absolute intolerance of the old grouch and the torture of being with him, day in, and day out."

At the university, they read the letters, chuckled, and wondered at the stubbornness of these two men, each quite nice in his own way, in their mutual dislike of each other.

They argued about how long the groundless feud would last. The optimists said both would finally make up and even come to like each other. The pessimists contended it would be just the opposite. There were several standing bets on the subject, and two quarrels.

A month later, however, a brief telegram from Kolguyev Island informed the university that Professor Burov had been murdered by Assistant Professor Voronov.

The special investigator in charge of the case began by looking for the means of reaching the island. Meteorological and other conditions, unfortunately, made the journey impossible at that time of the year.

The investigator then radioed instructions to the captain of an ice-breaker cruising near the island. The captain was to deliver the frozen corpse to Moscow, to interrogate the witnesses, if there were any, and most thoroughly search the site of the crime.

The investigator also demanded that Voronov be brought to Moscow with all due precautions.

The captain fulfilled his orders and entered the investigator's office some weeks later, accompanied by a man in his thirties with a lost and frightened expression.

The man was Voronov.

"Please be seated," the investigator said, looking him over with cold curiosity.

"Thank you," Voronov answered quietly.

The questioning began. The investigator carefully studied the records of Voronov's past.

In his thirty-two years he had lived honestly and well until the day he killed Burov. Voronov was a young but undoubtedly talented scientist. He had written several scientific papers and was firmly on the road to success.

"What, in God's name, made you kill the professor?" the investigator, usually a calm and self-controlled man, exclaimed. "What did you two fall out over?"

Voronov shrugged helplessly.

"You see," he said in an apologetic, hesitant, voice, "you see . . . the thing is, I didn't kill him at all."

"But he *was* killed?"

"Yes."

"Was there anyone at the scene of the crime except the two of you?"

"No, only the two of us! There was no one there, and no one could have possibly been. There can be no doubt about it."

"In that case, I can't see why you don't confess. You'll have to agree, that if two people are together and one of them is killed, the murderer. . ."

". . . can only be the other," Voronov put in. "It's undoubtedly so. But I did not kill him. The terrible thing about it is that I know the hopelessness of my situation. I have no chance in the world to defend myself. Of course, I've been—what is it they call it?—caught red-handed. If I were in your shoes, I'd never have a moment's doubt. I understand. I'm prepared for the worst. For the very worst. But I did *not* kill him."

And Voronov began to weep. He sobbed as strangely as he had spoken. This tall, calm, cultured man wept like a child, helplessly, without anger, and touchingly. He did not at all intend his tears to move his listener. But, on the other hand, he made no attempt to hide them. He wept as simply as he had spoken, and just as unaffectedly.

"Pull yourself together," the investigator admonished. "If you killed him—and everything seems to point to that—it's best to confess. If you did *not*, then defend yourself. Refute my arguments, explain your actions and present your side of the story."

The investigator said this, because Voronov's guilt seemed quite obvious. All the evidence pointed to the fact that Burov had been murdered by Voronov and no one else. But to the investigator's surprise, Voronov, far from trying to defend himself, provided additional and extremely incriminating information without the least prompting. While continuing to deny his guilt, he went on hurriedly to disclose new circumstances, facts and suppositions, all fatal to his case. Passionately and consistently he piled up the evidence against himself.

"When we came to the island," he said, "our animosity grew ever sharper. We tried to control our emotions, but our hatred entered every word, look and gesture. It was very difficult to keep oneself always in check; and that, unfortunately, did nothing to help the situation. Professor couldn't stand the sight of me, and I felt the same way about him. To tell you the truth, there were moments when I had half a mind to strike him, beat him up and even kill him. These thoughts began to torment me. They even found their way into my diary. I've brought it along. Here, have a look."

With these words Voronov handed the investigator a large note-book. True enough, among the other entries were those which showed that more and more often Voronov had kept playing with the thought of killing Professor Burov.

"I really don't know," he continued, "but perhaps in the end, when I'd no longer be able to control my emotions, I might actually have killed the professor. Perhaps! But I did *not* kill him. This is what happened.

"That morning we decided to go duck-shooting at a lake in the centre of the island. We went there by dog-sled. Our driver was a Nenets named Vasya. Half way there the sled broke. We had about two miles to go, and decided to continue on foot, while Vasya stayed to fix the sled.

"We arrived at the lake and began shooting. Then the ducks swam off to the far shore. I suggested that the professor remain where he was, while I went round to the other side to shoot from there. He agreed, and I set off for the opposite shore.

"As I stood there, a mile away, I had a clear view of the professor as he stood all alone on the opposite side. There was no one near him, and no one could have been. Of this I was sure. Then a shot rang out approximately where he was standing. I saw him jerk strangely and fall, and ran back to him, wondering what had happened.

"When I reached him he was still alive, but unconscious. There was a hunting knife plunged into his left eye to the very hilt which stuck out like a rotten swelling. His rifle lay beside him.

"I lost my head, not knowing what to do for the unfortunate man; I tried to pull the knife from his eye, but could not: it had been driven in with great force. Then I dashed back to where we had left the sled. Vasya was just finishing his repairs. I told him there had been a terrible accident and made him lash the dogs as hard as he could. By the time we reached the spot, the professor was dead. We took his body to camp, where we finally got the knife out of the eye with great difficulty. That's all. Do you mind if I smoke?"

"Not at all."

Voronov lit a cigarette, inhaling hungrily. After a brief pause he spoke again.

"So you see, it's hard for me to defend myself. I'm intelligent enough to see that everything in this case points to my guilt. In fact, I may even stand a better chance in court by confessing, by making a clean breast of it and sincerely repenting my crime, or whatever else you call it. I'm not a lawyer, but I've heard the term before. Yet, I cannot do that. I did *not* kill him. I did not do that, though I can't prove it. And I have only one request: these letters are from my fiancée, and this is a letter I've written to her. Will you please forward all of them to her?"

"No, I won't," the investigator replied. "You'd better give them to her yourself. I'm not going to arrest you, Voronov."

There are cases in which the unusual solution, the sudden conclusion and the final decision do not spring from a chain of formal clues and evidence, from the logical sequence of things already established and illuminated, from a final summary of the events. Often there are such dark and tangled labyrinths of facts, details and human relations, such a terrible piling up of all sorts of circumstantial evidence and chance occurrences that the most experienced investigator finds himself ready to throw up his hands. His guiding lights are his intuition and experience, his perseverence and conscience, his humaneness, the humaneness of a Soviet officer of the law—and these will surely lead him to the truth in the end.

The investigator put himself in a very awkward position by releasing Voronov. Voronov's guilt, on the one hand, seemed undeniable, as it evolved logically from the evidence of the case and seemed the only possible version. Besides, it was a well-founded version, one accepted by the circle informed of the case and understandably interested in it.

The freeing of Voronov, on the other hand, had been prompted solely by the investigator's intuition, by the fact that he had, for some reason or other, believed the man's story despite all proof to the contrary, the damning circumstances and facts. He had believed him and based his belief on those dim, vague and unclear grounds which are formed within the soul, which do not always appear to be logical on the surface, which are so difficult to express in words, which are never referred to, but which appear as a result of the investigator's skill, his psychological and professional insight, and the keenness of his intuition. They are the fruitful outcome of many years of thoughtful and tireless work, of training in observation, of experience in criminology, and of the constant habit of analyzing events and characters.

The investigator was convinced that Voronov had not murdered the professor. But he had to explain this, to prove it, and, what is more, to solve the mystery of Professor Burov's death. Voronov could not be cleared of all charges, only because the investigator was convinced of his innocence, no matter how positively.

Put in charge of the autopsy, P. Semyonovsky performed it with his usual skill and care and then reported his findings which boiled down to two points:

1. Professor Burov died as a result of extensive injuries caused by the blow of a hunting knife, plunged into the victim's left eye.

2. The blow was inflicted with a force greater than a human being's.

"What do you mean by 'greater than a human being's'?" the investigator asked. "How is one to understand that?"

"That means," the expert answered, "that the strength with which the blow was struck was greater than could be expected from an average person. That is why I used the words 'greater than a human being's.' But just how great that force was I cannot tell."

The investigator continued his work. He examined the professor's rifle. It was a Winchester and supplied nothing of interest to the case. The knife which inflicted the fatal blow was also quite ordinary; it was a rather cheap hunting knife with a wooden handle.

But examining it more closely, he discovered a small flaw in the handle, obviously the result of poor workmanship. The tiny end of the metal rod by which the handle was attached to the blade protruded as a sharp point from the wood, though it was barely noticeable.

The investigator ran his finger over the little piece of metal and suddenly sprang to his feet, as though burned by the thought that had flashed through his mind.

An hour later a group of hastily summoned experts, gunsmiths and hunters crowded the investigator's office.

"Tell me," he said to them, "what would a hunter do if he had a hunting knife with a wooden handle in his belt, and found that a cartridge had balked and got stuck in the magazine? For instance, if the cartridge became slightly enlarged from dampness or got bent, or was of an inferior quality—what would a hunter do then?"

Then experts exchanged surprised glances and began to whisper among themselves.

"In such a case," one said, when they had

finally come to a unanimous decision, "he would probably take his hunting knife and tap its smooth wooden handle on the capsule of the cartridge to prod it carefully in."

"That's what I thought, too," the investigator said and smiled. "Well, now, have a look at this knife. Please notice the little metal tip sticking out of the wood. Now, imagine that a hunter were to try to send the cartridge in with this knife. What do you think would happen?"

The experts examined the knife, noted the hard metal and reached agreement.

"This bit of metal," they said, "being as sharp and as strong as it is, could easily play the part of a firing pin. If this knife were used to tap the cartridge capsule, it might cause an explosion that would fire the rifle."

Then the investigator turned to the gunsmiths.

"Tell me," he said, "if the cartridge had not fully entered the magazine and if, as a result of the hunter's carelessness, the rifle were fired, where would the main force of the explosion be directed, and how great would that force be?"

"The force of the explosion would be directed backwards, throwing the hand holding the knife back to the face. The force of the shot would be very great, a pressure of five to seven atmospheres."

The investigator heaved a sigh of relief. His premonition had been correct.

Semyonovsky entered the office just then, and the investigator showed him the knife, repeating the experts' words.

"That's all very clever," Semyonovsky said slowly, "and even quite believable, if not for one small detail. The professor was killed by a blow to his left eye. According to your version, he could only have wounded himself in the right eye with his right hand, but never in the left one.

Then and there Semyonovsky calculated that, considering the length of the professor's arm, his height, and the correlation of various parts of his body, his right hand would have wounded him in the right eye if such a blow had occurred from the explosion, but never in the left.

The investigator's version which had seemed so clear and correct, was falling to pieces.

But he was a stubborn man, positive he had been right, and continued his research.

"Was the professor a healthy person?" he asked the dead man's relatives.

"Yes. Both physically and mentally," they answered.

"Was there anything peculiar about him? Did he have any handicaps?"

"No, there was nothing peculiar about him, and he had no handicaps."

"Did you ever see the professor use a scalpel?" the investigator persisted.

"Yes, certainly; he often worked at home."

"In which hand did he hold the scalpel?" he asked cautiously and even timidly, afraid that his last hope might vanish.

"Why, the professor was left-handed," came the calm reply.

The investigator could hardly keep from shouting for joy. There, finally, was the answer, the truth, the solution and the explanation! He had been left-handed! And off went the investigator to see Semyonovsky who sat down once again. Further calculation accurately showed that if the professor had placed the cartridge with his left hand, and it had gone off, he would most certainly have been struck in the left eye. Semyonovsky and the investigator then prepared a photo strip showing how the professor's left arm had moved when thrown back to his face and left eye by the force of the explosion.

Everything seemed clear at last. The truth had been uncovered; Professor Burov's death was explained, and Voronov was cleared completely. The case could have been closed now "for lack of evidence attesting to a crime." It could have been sent to the archives; and the investigator might have gone on to other cases waiting for him. Once again he would have wandered in the labyrinth of facts and human relationships, stumbling but always keeping on, making mistakes but also discoveries.

Yes, of course, but what about the knife? Where had the accursed knife come from?

Acquainted with the case, the professor's brother remarked.

"I'm ready to agree that you are right and that my brother died as a result of his own carelessness, but where did the knife come from? I'm also ready to state that he did not own such a knife. I know there was no such knife issued when they got their supplies. Whose knife was it? Whose could it be? And until you answer that question, Inspector, I cannot consider the case closed."

Professor Burov's brother was right in a way. His question certainly deserved an answer.

Voronov did not know where the professor had got the knife.

"I think," he said, "that it was professor Burov's knife. At any rate, I often saw him using such a knife."

The investigator went over the supply list. In the huge pile of bills, lists, receipts and reports, among the thousands of items, including shot, rifles, tents, canned goods, binoculars, pans, thermos bottles, axes, forks, pliers, hammers, metal cans, kerosene stoves, thermometers, dishes and many other things, the investigator searched in vain for an item marked: "Hunting knife—4 rubles."

Recalling that the expedition had sailed from Arkhangelsk after stopping there for several days, the investigator went to the procurator and asked to be sent to Arkhangelsk for a day.

"What for?" the procurator asked.

"For a knife," the investigator answered with a smile.

He arrived in Arkhangelsk on the next morning and hurried to the stores where he was shown hundreds of hunting knives, expensive and cheap, Finnish knives, knives from Vologda, Kostroma, Vyatka, and Pavlovo-Posad, but not one of the kind he was looking for. The salesmen eyed their fussy customer in dismay, the store managers shrugged, the cashiers giggled, but nowhere could he find the knife he wanted. Finally, towards evening, he wandered into a small shop of sporting goods on the Dvina Embankment. The first thing he noticed was a hunting knife with a wooden handle, an exact copy of the one that had killed the professor.

"How much does this knife cost?" the investigator asked nervously.

"Three seventy-five," the salesman answered.

The investigator summoned the manager and learned that only one co-operative made such knives, sending its entire output to this store. And yes, the knives had been on sale while the expedition was in Arkhangelsk.

"We sold many of them," the manager said, "and can't remember all our customers. Why should we?"

The investigator returned to Moscow. There, in Professor Burov's note-book, among hundreds of various entries, he found the following: "Arkhangelsk. Hunting knife—3 rub. 75 kop."

"Sit down, Comrade Voronov," the investigator said dryly. "This is the last time I've summoned you. Kindly read the order to close the case. Sign here, to show you've received a copy. Right over here."

Voronov took up the pen. Suddenly, everything seemed to swim before him—the pen, the inkwell and the face of the investigator sitting across the table.

But the investigator's words finally sank home. He realized that this horrible experience was now a thing of the past, that his innocence had been established and proved, that the truth had been discovered, and that the uncommunicative person sitting opposite him had saved his life and his honour.

1938

Mr. GROVER'S TRUE LOVE

The collective farmers of Glukhovo Village, Staritsky District, Kalinin Region probably still remember the strange event which took place on November 13, 1938. Late in the afternoon that day, a tiny, brightly painted foreign airplane suddenly darted out of the clouds and landed right in one of the fields. The pilot climbed out. Speaking Russian with a pronounced accent, he addressed the farmers gathered round the plane:

"Hello! I'm an Englishman and I've flown in from London. I've come to fetch my Russian fiancée."

"A likely story!" Aunt Sasha, the team leader whose son was the commander of an Air Force squadron cried impatiently. "Straight from London in such a mosquito! My, aren't you clever! Let me tell you, we're as smart as the rest about planes. All right, Mister bride-

189

groom, let's go over to the village Soviet. They'll look into the matter. Humph, as if they didn't have enough of their own girls, and he had to come flying over for one of ours!"

When militia officers were summoned by the village authorities, the stranger repeated his story to them: he was a British oil engineer, his name was Brian Montague Grover, he had previously worked in Grozny and Moscow, and had flown his little plane from London by way of Stockholm on a non-stop flight to the village of Glukhovo. He added that he had come to the Soviet Union without an appropriate visa in order to see the woman he loved and without whom his life was meaningless.

Next day Grover was taken to Moscow. In the investigator's office he gave a detailed account of the reasons which had prompted him to undertake the flight. Grover was a tall, fair-haired man with grey eyes that gazed frankly upon the world.

He began by saying that he, Brian Montague Grover, thirty-seven years of age and a native of Folkestone, understood that he had set out for the Soviet Union without a visa, knowing it was a criminal offence to do so, but that, unfortunately, he could not have done otherwise.

"I know all about Article 59-3d. I've learned it by heart and am ready to pay the penalty. I know that I may be sentenced to ten years in prison according to this article. But a British lawyer told me that another Article in the Soviet Criminal Code, namely, Article 51, can mitigate the first, and I think that this second article is most applicable in my case."

Grover spoke Russian fluently, though sometimes confusing his cases and conjugations. He had pleasant features, a firm mouth and strong teeth. As the investigator listened to his calm, unhurried story, he felt more and more confidence in the stranger, though he was obliged to ask him the usual questions, since the man had after all crossed the border illegally. Most disarming was the fact that he considered his arrest completely justified and was inwardly prepared to face the consequences, if "Article 51, didn't apply to the case."

He related the story of his love. When still a young though competent engineer back in the early thirties, he had found himself out of a job and accepted an offer to go to Grozny in the Soviet Union as a foreign specialist. He was attracted by the promise of a high salary, interesting work, and, finally, by the chance to see the mysterious and unknown "Soviet Russia" of which he had heard and read the most contradictory and vague reports.

He arrived in Moscow and stopped off at the Metropole, where there were Frenchmen and Germans, Americans and Swedes, Belgians and Englishmen. What a varied crowd they were! There were businessmen and tourists, experts and diplomats, special correspondents and professional spies, people of all ages, professions and political outlooks. Some expressed their dislike of the country quite openly and made light of the Soviet five-year plans. Others, on the contrary, admitted that despite everything, the Bolsheviks were fulfilling their plans, though it was a mystery on what funds, by what means or with what labour. The third group spoke with respect of the endeavours of a people who had decided to overcome the industrial backwardness of their vast country in a remarkably short time.

Grover became acquainted with these people; he listened to their arguments, and walked about the streets of Moscow, marvelling at the Saint Basil's Cathedral and the spaciousness of Red Square, the towers and walls of the ancient Kremlin, the crooked lanes off Arbat Street paved with cobblestones, the cabbies at the crossroads, and the charming women who were not very well dressed in those days, but were striking enough in their special Russian way.

In the street Grover met young people with Komsomol badges and found them pleasant and well brought up. None of them growled at him, or tried to sign him up as a "Comintern agent," to make him steal the British Crown Jewels or blow up Westminster Abbey. On the contrary, they readily answered the foreigner's questions, telling him how to get to the street he wanted and, as often as not, would see him there personally in the friendliest way.

And so, little by little, Brian Grover came to like the country, the ancient city and the people.

When he arrived in Grozny and began to work, he met with such warm hospitality, that in a few months he felt as if he had been living there for years, which accounted for the great number of friends he had made. This impression became especially strong after he had met Elena Golius, a pharmacist in one of the Grozny drug stores. He was immediately drawn to the quiet, dark-haired, pretty girl with a mischievous smile and the clear gaze of a person who had nothing to hide or be ashamed of in life.

Elena spoke a bit of English, though pronouncing the words incorrectly. Grover offered to teach her if she would agree to teach him Russian. Both were very good students.

A year later Grover could make himself understood in Russian, while Elena's pronunciation had improved markedly. Their relationship, however, had made even better progress. Elena's father, a pharmacist like his daughter, began to whisper anxiously to his wife about "that long-legged fellow spending too many evenings with our daughter." Elena's mother took the girl's side, timidly objecting that Brian Grover was a very nice boy; but her husband only coughed angrily, declaring quite logically that "there are plenty of marriageable boys in the U.S.S.R." and that he had not raised a daughter to have her die of consumption in London.

When his wife asked why he thought Elena would come down with consumption—after all, there were several million people living in London and very few of them had the disease —the old man explained that the English were used to their own climate, but that as soon as a Russian landed there he'd get it straight away.

"And then, again," he added, "one language is quite enough for two young people to pledge their love—just remember our own youth—but they speak two languages already. It won't come to any good, I tell you."

Her parents never dreamed that thousands of miles from Grozny, in far-away foggy London, another mother's heart was beating anxiously. Mrs. Grover, reading over her son's letters, noticed with alarm that the name of Elena was appearing ever more frequently.

When she received a snapshot of her son and a young woman with his jacket thrown over her shoulders, she examined it closely with a pang of the jealousy felt by every mother in the world whether in England or Russia, peasant woman or city woman, regardless of colour or the constellations overhead.

Soon Mrs. Grover puzzled her neighbourhood librarian by borrowing books exclusively by Russian authors. And they, alas, in no way calmed her fears: Anna Karenina had been unfaithful to her husband, although undoubtedly a gentleman; and as if that were not enough, she had thrown herself under a train. Sholokhov's Aksinya had also left her husband, but brought Grigory no happiness. Vera, in Goncharov's *Precipice*, for reasons unknown had rejected the love of the honourable Mister Raisky and given her heart to the most questionable Mister Volokhov. And, finally, even Pushkin's Tatyana had done such a shocking thing as to write a love letter to Mister Onegin, though he, Heaven knows, had certainly given her no reason to do so; thus, she had placed this most admirable young man in an awfully embarrassing position.

Ah, Russia was a land of mystery! And those Russian women, though they behaved strangely, had a very special charm!

"After completing my work in Grozny," Grover continued, "I was transferred to the Moscow Institute of Oil. Elena also moved to Moscow. My contract ended in 1934 and I returned to London. I wanted to come back to Russia, but there were no new contracts and I had no visa. Still, I realized I could not live without Elena."

It was then that he decided to fly to his beloved. He enrolled in a London flying club and learned to fly in several months. He began to save his money until he had enough to pay the hundred and seventy-three pounds needed for a second-hand Piper Cub. He took off from Brocksburn Airfield on November 3, 1938, his destination the U.S.S.R., with stops at Amsterdam, Bremen, Hamburg and Stockholm. From there he flew non-stop to the village of Glukhovo.

The news of this amazing event appeared in most papers of the world. I recall the headlines of the day: "Romance of the 20th Century," "On Wings of Love," "Englishman's Love Works Miracles," "Love Shatters Space."

On November 23rd the British press carried the news that the Conservative M. P. Cayzer intended to take the matter up in the House of Commons. On November 28, Reuters informed the world that the inquiry had been made and Sir Neville Chamberlain had informed Parliament that the British chargé d'affaires in Moscow had been instructed to discuss the matter with the Soviet Government.

The *Daily Telegraph and Morning Post* wrote that Grover had made his dangerous flight from Stockholm to Moscow under hazardous conditions.

The German fascist press carried a series of articles alleging that Grover faced the death penalty, "for the Communists are unable to understand the meaning of Love. Is it not a known fact that in the U.S.S.R. people fall in love according to orders issued by the trade-union committees? How then will they ever be able to understand Grover and his truly Shakespearian emotions? No, Red Moscow is no haven for modern Romeos and Juliets!"

Another view was expressed by a British lawyer:

"Yes, Moscow has every legal right to try Brian Grover. Love and the law—what an old, yet eternally new problem! An article of the Soviet Criminal Code and a young heart beating passionately, full of love! Would not the sternest judge soften at the sight of this tragic conflict? We refuse to believe that Grover's trial will end in tragedy and are optimistically awaiting the outcome."

Meanwhile, Elena Golius was questioned to verify the facts of Grover's story. Both versions coincided completely. She was then informed that he had flown to the Soviet Union and that she would be allowed to see him immediately. When he, in turn, was told that he would see his Elena in a few moments, his usually calm face turned pale. He bit his lower lip and lit a cigarette.

He was left in the room with an assistant while the investigator went to fetch Elena.

Grover rushed to her when she came in, and they embraced, laughing and whispering, laughing through their tears again and whispering again.

And if anything was unclear to the investigator now, it was only what Brian Grover had whispered to Elena.

Perhaps, he had told her of his take-off from the Brocksburn Airfield that dreary November morning and of his flight from Stockholm over the sullen restless Baltic Sea to Moscow? Of the miles rushing by beneath the wings of his little plane, of the icy blasts of wind that shook it, while he kept on and on, clutching at the wheel, flying towards the glow of her brown eyes as towards a beacon, towards the only eyes that existed for him as inimitable as life, happiness and love? Or perhaps he had told her how he had missed her and that, come what may, he was happy just to sit by her side now and hold her little hand in his? Or that his mother had asked him to kiss Elena and tell her that an English mother thanked this Russian girl for the love she had brought her son, that she was happy for her, and even a bit jealous? Or that though they had been born under different skies and had spoken their first

words in different languages, they had nonetheless found a mutual tongue?

The case was heard in the Moscow City
Court on December 31, 1938. The entire staff
of the British Embassy was present at the hear-
ing of the case of "Brian Montague Grover, a
British subject born in the city of Folkestone
in 1901, charged under Article 59-3d of the
Criminal Code of the R.S.F.S.R." Diplomats with
monocles, their wives with gold lorgnettes,
British and American correspondents, and
the various attachés were all in attendance.

The small and modest courtroom had never
before seen such a grand gathering. Rolls-
Royces and Buicks belonging to the diplomatic
corps glittered at the entrance.

The presiding judge, a blond, blue-eyed man
with a kindly face, and the two People's As-
sessors, both women in red kerchiefs—one an
elderly textile worker from the Trekhgornaya
Factory and the other a young worker of the
Electric Plant—entered from the judge's chambers and sat down at the red-covered table. A
hush fell on the courtroom, as the public
looked with interest at the judges' table, Lenin's
portrait and the simple, unpretentious fur-
nishings.

There was no statue of Themis holding the scales, no crucifixes, no marble columns, no policemen in dress uniforms, no imposing emblems of justice. The judges wore no black silk robes with heavily starched white collars, no gold chains and powdered wigs. There were no sleek faced, illustrious jurors in black morning coats and starched shirt fronts, no venomous procurator with his sarcastic questions and granite profile, no stern bailiffs, no saucy stenographers with stylish coiffures—none of these!

But in this simple courtroom, in the earnest and thoughtful eyes of the judges, in their frank and kindly faces, and in the simple judicial procedure bereft of theatrical pomp, there was something hitherto unseen by this public, something which commanded involuntary respect and trust and explained why this court, for the first time in history, had earned the right to be called a people's court.

"The Court is in session," the presiding judge quietly proclaimed. "At the defendant's request, he is being represented by barrister Kommodov, a member of the Moscow Lawyers' Collegium."

Three hours later, having listened attentively to the testimony of the defendant and his lawyer, the judges retired to their chambers. The courtroom buzzed. Brian Grover, who had just told the Soviet judges the story of his love for a Russian girl, of her love for him, and of how he had illegally crossed the border and entered the U.S.S.R. because of this love, had said in conclusion:

"Honourable judges, I have told you the whole truth. What I now have to say I would like to say in Russian, though I have an interpreter. I wish to do this because I have come to love your country and your people as I love my dear Elena. I lived in Russia for several years, working and spending my leisure time with Russians. The ocean of your labour contains the small drop I have contributed, and I am proud of this. Yes, I lived and worked with Russians, I laughed and sang with them, and I would consider it an honour to become related to these people. That is all I have to say."

Then the judges left to confer, and the courtroom buzzed. Grover awaited the outcome calmly, not afraid that these ordinary Russian people now deciding his fate had not understood him. He thought that if all

202

the problems in the world were decided by such ordinary English, Russian, American and German people, no one would ever know fear again.

A bell rang and the judges returned. The presiding judge read the sentence. Brian Grover had violated the Soviet border by illegally flying to the U.S.S.R. In accordance with Article 59-3d of the Criminal Code of the Republic, the Court found him guilty of this crime.

"However," the presiding judge continued, "the Court cannot overlook the reasons behind the crime and considers it an established fact that the defendant is sincerely in love with a Soviet woman, who, on her part, shares his feelings. Their love has passed the test of time and separation and is therefore to be respected. It alone prompted the defendant to fly to the U.S.S.R. On the basis of Article 51 of the Criminal Code, the Court sentences Brian Grover to one month imprisonment or a fine of 1,500 rubles."

The judge's words were greeted with applause which was echoed throughout Great Britain that evening when the Moscow Court decision was broadcast over the radio.

Three days later, Grover and his wife Elena, after receiving the necessary visas, left for London.

Once again the papers were full of the news. The January 6, 1939 issue of the *Daily Telegraph and Morning Post* wrote that the moral of the story is that the Soviet Government can be very humane. The same paper printed Grover's statement on his arrival in London: "The trial held in connection with my illegal entry into the U.S.S.R. was conducted with complete honesty and justice."

Thus, the case ended. Seventeen years have elapsed since then. I know nothing of the fate of Mr. Grover, his wife and their children, if they have any. But I vividly remember their faces, their meeting, their excited and happy whispering and the story of their love.

As a criminologist, I would like to add that the love of these two people, established as a fact in the court's verdict, which is law, since the defendant did not appeal against it, must therefore be regarded as proven beyond doubt, irrevocably and forever.

That is why I should like to wish Brian Montague Grover, his wife and their children, which they must certainly have, in view of their persistent natures and mutual good-will, much happiness.

And, finally, I may add that the widespread notion that criminologists come up only against the shady sides of life is quite wrong.

1956